THE
US CONGRESS
☆ FOR KIDS ☆

THE US CONGRESS

FOR KIDS ★

Over 200 Years of Lawmaking,
Deal-Breaking, and Compromising

WITH 21 ACTIVITIES

Ronald A. Reis ★ Foreword by Rep. Henry A. Waxman ★ Afterword by Rep. Kristi Noem

CHICAGO
REVIEW
PRESS

First edition

Published by Chicago Review Press, Incorporated

814 North Franklin Street

Chicago, Illinois 60610

ISBN 978-1-61374-977-7

Library of Congress Cataloging-in-Publication Data

Reis, Ronald A.

   The US Congress for kids : over 200 years of lawmaking, deal-breaking, and compromising, with 21 activities / Ronald A. Reis ; foreword by Henry A. Waxman ; afterword by Kristi Noem.

         pages cm. — (For kids series)

   Summary: "With a focus on dramatic stories, personalities, and turning points, and accompanied by educational, hands-on activities, The US Congress for Kids helps children understand how the government functions and why it matters"—Provided by publisher.

   ISBN 978-1-61374-977-7 (paperback)

   1. United States. Congress—Juvenile literature. 2. Legislative bodies—United States—Juvenile literature. 3. Legislative power—United States—Juvenile literature. 4. Creative activities and seat work—Juvenile literature. I. Title.

   JK1025.R45 2014
   328.73—dc23

                                                                            2014017480

Cover and interior design: Monica Baziuk

Interior illustrations: Jim Spence

Cover images (Front, clockwise from top): Capitol building, Library of Congress LC-USZ62-121528; Portrait of Jeannette Rankin, Library of Congress LC-cph 3a11030; Senator Sam Ervin chairs the Senate Select Committee, Wally McNamee/CORBIS; Congresswoman Shirley Chisholm announcing her candidacy for the presidential nomination, WL008829; (RM) US-POLITICS-OBAMA-STATE OF THE UNION, 161726936; Senator Chuck Grassley, Courtesy of Chuck Grassley. (Back, left to right) Five students were detained after staging a sit-in at US Senator John McCain's office in support of the DREAM Act, courtesy Wikimedia Commons; Judge Bork, Bettmann/CORBIS U87308102; Senator Elizabeth Warren, Courtesy of Senator Elizabeth Warren; US Senate in Chaos, Library of Congress LC-DIG-ppmsca-29117; A group of activists at the National American Woman Suffrage Association parade held in Washington, DC, March 3, 1913, Library of Congress LC-DIG-ggbain-11400; Illustration by Jim Spence.

Printed in the United States

5 4 3 2 1

CONTENTS

ACKNOWLEDGMENTS

Thank you to LaVergne Rosow and Lauren Okayama for your helpful activity suggestions. Thank you Dale Beck, my first editor, who is always there. Thank you Ellen Hornor, editorial assistant at Chicago Review Press, for your quick responses to my inquiries. And, of course, a special thanks to Lisa Reardon, senior editor at Chicago Review Press, for all your encouragement and professionalism. Finally, a special debt of gratitude to my wife, Karen, for all you do in aiding my writing efforts.

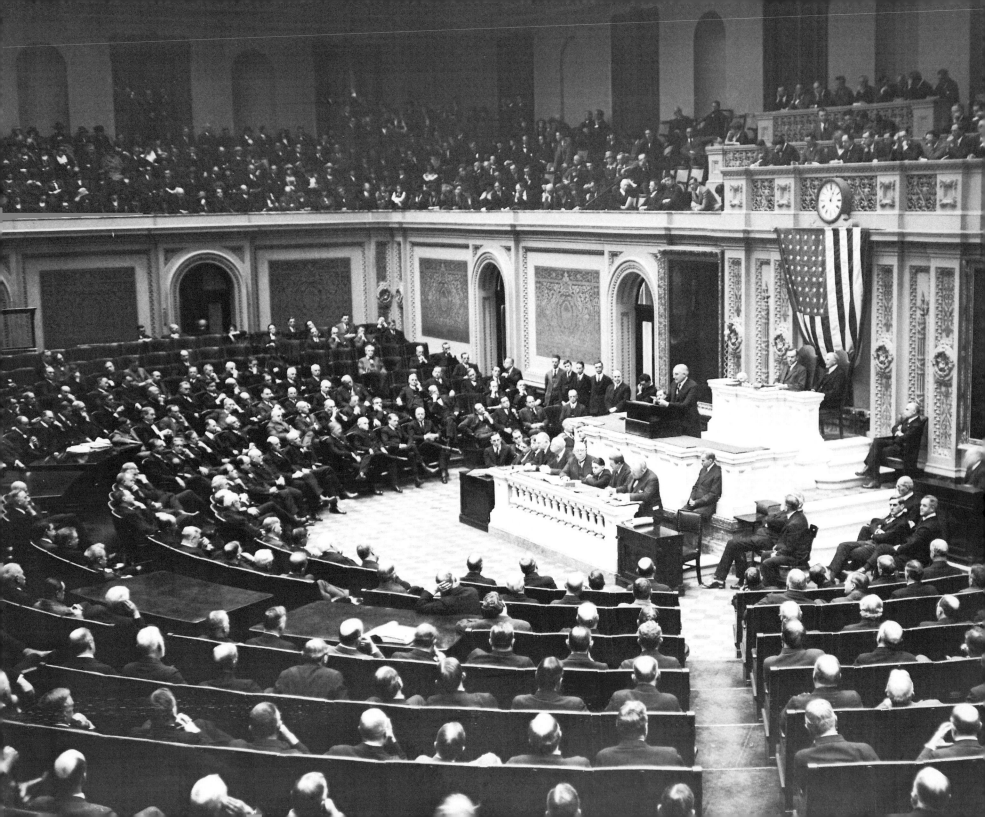

FOREWORD

It's an exciting time to learn about Congress and our government. Congress truly is a body of the people, by the people, and for the people. Together, members of Congress represent the entire nation, bringing with them a range of diverse backgrounds, interests, and experiences to make decisions on behalf of the American people.

The Constitution confers great power upon Congress to govern. Throughout history, the work of the Congress has greatly changed the nation. It abolished slavery and created new federal programs under President Roosevelt's New Deal to bring the country out of the Great Depression. It passed civil rights laws to end racist practices and established environmental protections to guarantee the safety of the air we breathe and the water we drink. It changed the landscape of national security after September 11 and passed landmark health care reform to provide better health care to all Americans.

Many of the most important figures in our nation's history have been members of Congress. Approximately half of this country's presidents served in Congress. Many members of the Cabinet, including secretaries of state, served in Congress. Even Davy Crockett was a member of Congress from Tennessee.

The legislature is the branch of government that most directly allows you to participate and have your voice heard. Your member of Congress carries your voice to Washington and fights for you and your families. When you begin voting at age 18, you can choose the best candidate to represent your interests. And when you turn 25, you can run for Congress yourself and make important choices for your country.

FORMER CONGRESSMAN HENRY A. WAXMAN served for 40 years in the House of Representatives, representing Los Angeles's Westside. The congressman was known as a tireless author of bills and negotiator of deals. He retired with the end of the 113th Congress, effective January 2, 2015.

INTRODUCTION

Opinion poll after opinion poll continues to show that the majority of Americans do not like their Congress very much. When questioned about their individual representative or **senator**, they are less inclined to be critical; they feel the man or woman they have sent to Congress is doing an OK job. Not a great job—an OK job. Of the three branches of **government**—the legislative (Congress), executive (the president and all agencies under his or her control), and judicial (the courts)—it is the legislative, the one that makes the **laws**, that gets the lowest approval ratings. And yet, our **founding fathers** considered Congress to be the most important of the three branches. That is why they listed it first when crafting the US Constitution.

This book has been written in the hopes of showing you, despite all the criticism, what an amazing institution Congress is. For 225 years it has given us the democracy we cherish. It was there to overthrow slavery, challenge executive branch authority, give women the right to vote, make major strides in civil rights, and provide the necessary advice and consent rulings, among many other major achievements. As you will see, the working of Congress has never been smooth. With so much national diversity on so many issues, it is unrealistic to expect that lawmaking would proceed on an orderly path. Congress, as a representative institution, reflects our messy, confrontational lives. Yet, the alternative is an authoritarian form of government that freedom-loving people will never endorse. If, in completing this book, you gain a better understanding of the US Congress along with an appreciation for the positive good it has done, you will be on your way to becoming better equipped to understand American history as it unfolds today.

Capitol Hill is in the center of the picture, with congressional office buildings to the right and the left. Library of Congress LC-DIG-highsm-4879

TIME LINE

1789	March 4—First US Congress meets in New York City
1789	First Congress passes 12 amendments to the Constitution, 10 of which are ratified by 1791, becoming the Bill of Rights
1800	Lawmakers hold the first session of Congress inside the new Capitol building in Washington, DC
1814	During the War of 1812, the British burn the Capitol, the White House, and other buildings
1819	The Supreme Court case *McCulloch v. Maryland* upholds the "implied powers of Congress"
1830	The "Great Debate" over states rights in the Senate grips the Congress and the nation
1857	The House of Representatives moves into its current home in the south wing of the Capitol
1859	The Senate moves into its current home in the enlarged north wing of the Capitol
1865	Congress passes the 13th Amendment abolishing slavery
1868	For the first time, the House of Representatives impeaches a president, Andrew Johnson
1870	Senator Hiram Revels, a Mississippi Republican, becomes the first African American to serve in Congress

1897	Library of Congress building opens
1906	Congress passes the Meat Inspection Act and the Pure Food and Drug Act, establishing government regulation over the food industry
1913	The 16th Amendment to the Constitution, authorizing an income tax, becomes the law of the land
1913	The 17th Amendment to the Constitution, authorizing the direct election of senators, becomes the law of the land
1916	Jeannette Rankin of Montana becomes the first woman elected to Congress
1919	The 18th Amendment to the Constitution, prohibiting the sale of alcoholic beverages, becomes the law of the land

1920	With the passage of the 19th Amendment to the Constitution, women are allowed to vote in national elections
1932	Hattie Wyatt Caraway of Arkansas becomes the first woman to enter the Senate by election
1933	The 21st Amendment is passed, nullifying the 18th Amendment
1953	Joseph McCarthy chairs a Senate committee on communist influence in the government
1957	Senator Strom Thurmond of South Carolina speaks for more than 24 hours straight, attempting to filibuster (block) the 1957 Civil Rights Act
1964	The Civil Rights Act of 1964 passes Congress
1965	The Voting Rights Act of 1965 passes Congress
1969	Shirley Chisholm is sworn in as the first black woman to be elected to Congress
1991	Clarence Thomas is confirmed as a US Supreme Court justice
1995	The Republican Party wins control of both houses of Congress for the first time since 1954
1998	The House of Representatives votes to impeach President Bill Clinton

1999	The Senate votes to acquit President Clinton of charges in his impeachment
2001	Al Qaeda terrorists crash three planes into the World Trade Center and the Pentagon on September 11
2002	Congress passes a joint resolution to authorize the use of US armed forces against Iraq
2005	Congress begins investigation of performance-enhancing drugs in American sports
2007	Nancy Pelosi becomes the first woman Speaker of the House of Representatives
2009	Barack Obama is inaugurated (installed) as America's first black president
2010	Republicans gain control of the House of Representatives
2013	Congress allows automatic budget cuts, known as the sequester, to go into effect on January 3
2013	October 1, government shuts down as Congress fails to reach spending agreement
2014	April 2, the Supreme Court strikes down campaign donor limitations; wealthy individuals are now able to give a total of $3.6 million to congressional candidates

Slaves taken from a captured ship.
Library of Congress LC-DIG-ppmsca-15836

★ 1 ★

UNFINISHED BUSINESS
Congress and Slavery

Preston Brooks, a member of the House of Representatives from South Carolina, was determined to choose his weapon carefully. After some consideration, the 36-year-old congressman settled upon a dog cane, a light instrument used to discipline unruly canines. But Brooks planned to take the stick to a human being who, in his anger, he felt to be lower than any animal on Earth.

On the morning of May 21, 1856, Brooks arrived at the nation's **capital**, Washington. Carrying his gold-headed dog stick, the young congressman sought a 45-year-old senator from Massachusetts, Charles Sumner. He could not locate him.

The following day, Brooks entered the **Capitol** Building and walked into the **Senate chamber**. There, Sumner sat at his desk, signing envelopes containing copies of his "The Crime Against Kansas" speech that he had delivered over

1

a two-day period, on May 19 and 20. Brooks calmly walked to Sumner's desk.

"You have libeled my state and slandered my relation, who is aged and absent," Brooks declared. "I feel it to be my duty to punish you."

The beating Senator Sumner took from Brooks would leave him permanently injured. As a result, the senator spent an astonishing three years away from the Congress he loved, recuperating. Nonetheless, Charles Sumner eventually returned to the Senate, where he served for another 18 years.

Why did this beastly act occur? Why did a member of the House of Representatives attack a US senator with the intent to cripple if not kill him?

In his "The Crime Against Kansas" speech, Sumner, an antislavery Republican, had torn into two proslavery advocates, one of whom was Senator Andrew Butler from South Carolina. "Of course he has chosen a mistress to whom he has made his vows, and who, though ugly to others, is always lovely to him," Sumner declared on the Senate **floor**. "Though

★ THE THREE-FIFTHS CLAUSE ★

It was known as the shameful three-fifths clause, and it was written right into the US **Constitution**, where it would remain until passage of the 14th Amendment, on July 9, 1868. Slaves would be counted not as full human beings, but as only three-fifths of a person. Yet the clause is known as "shameful" not because of any moral worth of black persons, as is often assumed. Rather it was considered disgraceful because such persons were counted at all.

The number of House of Representative seats in Congress is allocated to each state on the basis of its population. Various formulas have been used over the years to determine how many seats each state gets. Naturally, a given state wants as many seats as possible. Since the number of seats is determined by how many people reside in a given state, counting everyone is every state's goal. When the Constitution was written in 1787, the question of whether to count slaves or not took center stage.

The free states of the North did not want slaves to count at all. Since slaves had no legal rights and never would, they were irrelevant to the process of representation, it was argued. They should go uncounted.

The slave states of the South countered that slaves should count as full persons. They contributed materially to the national prosperity, it was said. Government was about protection of property as well as the personal rights of citizens.

As a compromise, it was decided that each slave would count as three-fifths of a person. Today, the three-fifths clause is often interpreted as an insult to black slaves. The slave states wanted them to count as full persons to give their states more representatives. Slave interests, of course, would in no way be represented. On the contrary, giving slaves a full count would actually enhance the power of slave owners to defend the institution of slavery.

polluted in the sight of the world, is chaste [pure] in his sight. I mean the harlot [prostitute] slavery."

It so happened that Andrew Butler was the uncle of Preston Brooks. The elderly Butler was not present during Sumner's speech, having earlier suffered a stroke. He lay recuperating in South Carolina.

In attendance, however, was Senator Stephen Douglas of Illinois, also the subject of criticism during Sumner's speech. Douglas had leaned over to a colleague and whispered, "This damn fool [Sumner] is going to get himself shot by some other damn fool."

The national reaction to the beating of Senator Sumner broke along regional lines. In the South, Brooks was hailed as a hero for upholding the honor of his family and the South as a whole. The congressman was sent dozens of new canes, one of them inscribed with the words "Good Job."

Though Brooks was censured (condemned) by the House of Representatives and, as a result, resigned, he was immediately reelected. The congressman died soon thereafter, however, from a liver ailment, in January 1857. Preston Brooks was 37 years old.

The breakdown of reasoned debate that the beating of Senator Sumner symbolized continued. In four years the country would plunge into civil war over the issue of slavery.

African American men, women, and children being auctioned off in front of a crowd.
Library of Congress LC-cph 3a6254

A Short-Lived Victory

DURING THE battle for independence, in mid-1776, the 13 British colonies, through their Continental Congress, drafted the Articles of Confederation. The Articles proved to be a weak form of government. They provided for no executive, no judiciary, and a virtually powerless Congress. Six years after the war ended, in 1787, a convention was called to revise the Articles of Confederation. It was soon realized, however, that a whole new form of government was required. It was at this Philadelphia Convention, over a four-month period, that a new

Constitution was drafted. On March 4, 1789, the new government, formed by the recently (1788) **ratified** (formally approved) Constitution, would be installed.

The US Constitution included a curious provision on the abolition (elimination) of the slave trade. The stipulation, in Article I, Section 9, of the Constitution, prevented any interference in such trade before the year 1808:

The Migration or Importation of such Persons as any of the States now existing shall think proper to admit, shall not be prohibited by the Congress prior to the Year one thousand eight hundred and eight, but a Tax or duty may be imposed on such Importation, not exceeding ten dollars for each Person.

The South, consisting of slaveholding states, was elated. General Charles Cotesworth Pinckney, of South Carolina, bragged that the "South had won a great victory" in protecting the slave trade for at least 20 years.

Furthermore, Pinckney and other members of Congress realized that the clause did not require an end to the slave trade in 1808. To actually terminate the trade would require passing a **bill** in both chambers of Congress, the House and the Senate. It would then need to be signed by the president.

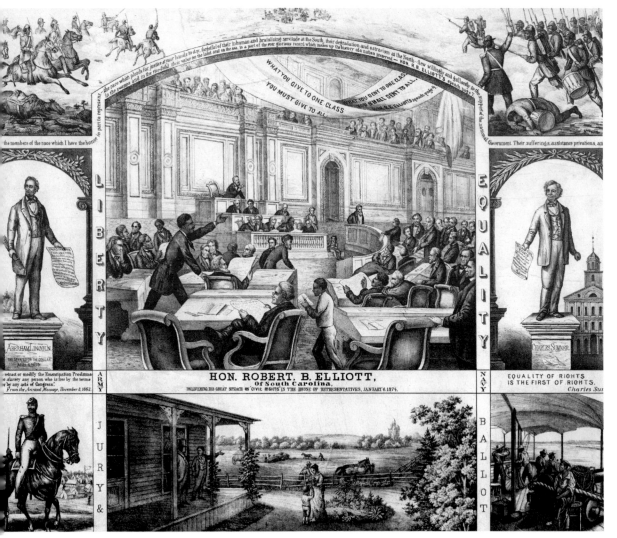

A series of illustrations celebrating the end of slavery, including one of South Carolina Representative Robert B. Elliott's famous 1874 speech in favor of the Civil Rights Act (center). Library of Congress LC-DIG-pga-2595

On March 2, 1807, the US Congress did exercise its constitutional power to halt the international slave trade. President Thomas Jefferson promptly signed the Act to Prohibit the Importation of Slaves, making it law. The Constitution, however, required that the effective date be delayed until January 1, 1808.

It must be pointed out that this act did not end slavery in the United States. The widespread trade of slaves within the South was not prohibited. The Southern states went along with the elimination of the international slave trade in part because by 1808 they had a self-sustaining population of over four million captives. With the children of slaves automatically becoming slaves themselves, the South was assured of a never-ending secure supply of human property.

Though slavery in the United States was to continue in the decades to come, the Act to Prohibit the Importation of Slaves was a milestone. According to historian William Freechling, the act to end the slave trade was "probably the most important slavery legislation Congress ever passed and among the most important American laws on any subject."

The Congressional Gag Rule

ON DECEMBER 20, 1837, William Slade, a congressman from the northern state of Vermont, rose in the House of Representatives to give a speech on the abolition of slavery and the slave trade in the District of Columbia. In doing so, the congressman certainly had no desire to offend. Yet in speaking on the subject of slavery, on the floor of Congress, Slade had violated a new House of Representatives rule

In this 1870 illustration, the artist envisions African Americans enjoying advances in education and science after passage of the 15th Amendment granting them the right to vote.
Library of Congress LC-DIG-pga-2587

5

Find Your Representative

REPRESENTATIVES are members of the House of Representatives. They are also called congressmen and congresswomen. There are 435 representatives, and no matter where in the United States you live, one of them represents you. In this activity you will learn more about your representative and your congressional district.

Materials
* Access to a computer with a printer
* Highlighter pen (a light color is best)
* Manila file folder

1. Go to the website Contacting the Congress: A Citizen's Congressional Directory, at www.contactingthecongress.org. Fill out the address form to determine who your representative is. Click on his or her name and print out the information about your representative.

2. Highlight the following:
* The Congressional District number and state
* Your representative's political party
* His or her leadership position, if any
* Your representative's status as a freshman
* Your representative's Washington, DC, mailing address
* Your representative's District Office(s) address
* Your representative's web homepage

3. Click on your representative's web homepage. Once you arrive at his or her site, search for a map of your district. Most representatives have a button indicating their district map. If you cannot find the district map on your representative's home webpage, go to Google and type in "map of xx (for example, 29th) congressional district, state (for example, California).

4. Print out the map of your congressional district. Using your highlighter, color in your district on the map and locate, as best you can, your residence. Mark it on the map.

5. Place all your printouts in a folder and label it "My Representative." Save your folder to be used for further activities.

maintaining that a discussion about slavery and abolition was too quarrelsome for debate. In raising the issue, Slade drove Southerners right out of the hall.

In early March of the previous year, John C. Calhoun, the fiery, unyielding senator from South Carolina, had warned Congress against interfering in any way with the South's system of slave labor, its "**peculiar institution**." "The relations which now exist between the two races," he said, "has existed for two centuries. It has grown with our growth and strengthened with our strength. It has entered into and modified all our institutions, civil and political. We will not, can not, permit it to be destroyed."

Nearly 58 years earlier, when the government was being created in 1790, another South Carolinian, William Smith, had put the issue more directly. "We took each other, with our mutual bad habits and respective evils," he reminded his colleagues, "for better, for worse; the Northern States adopted us with our slaves, and we adopted them with their Quakers." As far as Smith and other Southerners were concerned, discussion of slavery was, in today's jargon, "a nonstarter."

Yet by the mid-1830s, petitions from northern abolitionists began pouring into Congress—by the thousands. Many of these petitioners agreed that Congress had no power to abolish slavery in the states where it then existed without a constitutional **amendment**. However, reasoned the petitioners, since Congress created the District of Columbia (DC) (the seat of the federal government sandwiched between the two slave states of Maryland and Virginia) and had exclusive jurisdiction over its affairs, Congress could outlaw slavery within.

Congressman Slade agreed. "What do the petitioners ask at our hands?" he intoned in that December 27 speech to his fellow representatives. "Why, sir, simply that measures may be taken to put an end to slavery here, and especially that here, where the flag of freedom floats over the Capitol of this great Republic, and where the authority of that Republic is supreme, the trade in human flesh may be abolished. These are the questions which gentleman are called on to meet, but which they do not meet, either by calling the petitioners 'ignorant fanatics' or denouncing them as 'murderers and incendiaries [burners of property].'"

Southerners would have none of it! To them, for Congress to even raise the issue was unacceptable.

Nonetheless, to petition Congress was a basic right of citizenship, written into the US Constitution. To deny citizens the right to be heard was a violation of their civil liberties.

In response to the flood of petitions, proslavery forces in Congress passed a series of "gag rules" that automatically "tabled" all such petitions. In doing so, the petitions would never be read or discussed.

The gag rules angered Americans from northern states. Massachusetts congressman John Quincy Adams declared that they violated the First Amendment right "to petition the Government for redress of grievances." Petitions from the North, demanding the abolition of slavery in the District of Columbia, dramatically increased. The issue of slavery and its abolition would not go away.

John C. Calhoun as he looked in 1850.

Write a Letter to Your Representative

It may seem quaint, even old-fashioned, to be writing to your congressperson. But doing so on an issue you care about can be extremely effective. Whether you choose to send a message via e-mail or snail mail (paper with envelope and stamp), the letter will have impact if it is written correctly. Writing a letter is a skill that will improve with practice. Below are the steps to take in writing an effective, attention-getting, response-generating letter to your congressional representative.

Materials
★ Access to a computer with a printer
★ Paper, envelope, stamp, etc., if sending a hard copy

1. Determine why you are writing the letter. Do you have a strong opinion on a national issue in the news? Do you feel you have been treated unfairly by an agency of the federal government? Does a particular law being considered by Congress seem unfair to you? Are you working on the Citizenship in the Nation Merit Badge for the Boy Scouts? Make sure you are writing about an issue a member of the House of Representatives is in a position to deal with.

2. Determine whether your letter will be sent by e-mail or as a hard copy. The hard copy letter will have more impact, but, given the security issues in sending mail to Congress, you may want to write via e-mail. Either way, the letter should be the same in style and substance.

3. Open your letter with the appropriate address and salutation (an expression of greeting). Here is an example:

> *The Honorable John Q. Smith*
> *US House of Representatives*
> *111 Address*
> *Washington, DC 20010*
> *Dear Representative Smith:*

4. Keep your letter short—no more than one page is best.

5. Identify yourself in the first sentence. ("My name is Linda Wright and I am in the fifth grade at John F. Kennedy Elementary School in Evergreen, California.")

6. Be polite and respectful. Above all, do not include anything that could be construed as a threat.

7. Get straight to the point. After you have identified yourself, summarize why you are writing and what it is you want. Be specific. Do not ramble on. If you are writing about a particular bill, provide the name and number if possible (for example, "USA PATRIOT Act HR 3162").

8. Back up your concerns with as many facts and statistics as you can. Also, if you can include a personal story that is relevant, do so. This will help "bring the message home." But remember, be factual, not emotional.

9. Be sure to include your name and complete address, even in an e-mail.

Conclude your letter as follows:

> *Sincerely,*
> *Your Name*
> *Your Title (if appropriate)*
> *Your Address*
> *Your Phone Number*

10. Ask for (but do not demand) a response. Hopefully you will receive a reply. But remember, even if you don't get an answer, it doesn't mean you haven't been heard.

Congressional Venom

IT WASN'T that Congress was unwilling to compromise over slavery. Indeed, three major compromises, each 30 years apart, attempted to pacify pro- and antislavery regions of the country.

The first, known as the Compromise of 1790, involved founding fathers Thomas Jefferson, Alexander Hamilton, and James Madison. In June 1790, the three met for dinner and worked out a deal that Congress would later approve. The capital of the United States would be moved from Philadelphia to the Potomac, to become Washington, DC. In exchange, the federal government would assume debts acquired by the states during the Revolutionary War. The South liked the compromise because it put

ABOVE: **Union soldiers with rifles at attention in front of the Capitol.**
Library of Congress LC-cph 3b3289

LEFT: **Henry Clay was a giant of the US Congress.**
Library of Congress LC-DIG-pga-46

the nation's capital between two slave states—Maryland and Virginia.

The Missouri Compromise of 1820, brokered to a large extent by Senator Henry Clay of Kentucky, was an effort by both chambers of Congress to maintain a balance between slaveholding states and free states. With new western territories becoming states, it was agreed that some would be free and others slave. Though the Missouri Compromise may have temporarily eased arguments over the question of slavery, it served notice that the South not only had no intention of ending slavery, it wanted to expand it—westward.

The Compromise of 1850, where Henry Clay again played a decisive role, also dealt with slavery in the new territories. It was another balancing act. Among other features, in exchange

A symbolic group portrait praising recent legislative efforts, notably the Compromise of 1850, to preserve the Union.
Library of Congress LC-DIG-pga-261

for abolishing the slave trade (though not slavery itself) in Washington, DC, the South got a stronger Fugitive Slave Act. The latter required the North to return runaway slaves.

Though congressional compromises held off disunion for a while, they did not succeed in preventing the inevitable—the breakup of the United States through civil war.

The decade of the 1850s saw both regions of the country, North and South, becoming more isolated from one another, suspicious of each other's motives, and vengeful toward those who represented each region's interests. Congress, as would be expected, was home to all the anger and hatred on a personal level that such distrust generated.

With the election of Abraham Lincoln as president of the United States in November 1860, it took only a month for South Carolina to secede from the Union. Other southern states soon followed. On April 12, 1867, Confederate forces fired on Fort Sumter, a federal installation in South Carolina. The Civil War had begun.

One year later, on April 16, 1861, in the midst of the ongoing struggle, Congress voted, without Southern participation, to eliminate slavery in the District of Columbia. Unfinished business finally finished.

★ ★ ★ ★ ★ ★ ★ ★ ★ ★

★ AARON BURR ★

It has been said that if Aaron Burr had kept his ambition and ego in check, he would have become president of the United States. Instead, he is known to history as the man who killed founding father Alexander Hamilton.

That Burr was brilliant, there is no doubt. At the age of 13, in 1769, he entered what was then called the College of New Jersey but is known today as Princeton University. Burr graduated at age 17.

Burr fought in the Revolutionary War, achieving the rank of major. In 1791, he entered politics, obtaining a seat in the US Senate by beating General Philip Schuyler, Alexander Hamilton's father-in-law. It is at this point that the lifelong animosity between Burr and Hamilton most likely began.

In the complex and confusing presidential election of 1800, Aaron Burr wound up vice president of the United States, while Thomas Jefferson became president. Burr believed it was he who should have won the highest office and that, through Hamilton's maneuvering, he was denied it. The feud between the two intensified.

Though he was also a vice president, Aaron Burr is more famous for killing Alexander Hamilton in a duel.
Library of Congress LC-cph 3a1932

At the close of his term as vice president, Burr ran for governor of New York, but lost. He again blamed Hamilton, who he accused of besmearing him as a candidate. Eager to defend his honor, Burr challenged Hamilton to a duel. It has been suggested that Burr hoped Hamilton would decline the invitation, but he did not. On July 11, 1804, on the dueling grounds at Weehawken, New Jersey, Burr shot Hamilton to death.

In New Jersey, Burr was charged with murder. Yet, incredibly, he was let off. Even more unbelievably, Burr was allowed to complete his vice presidential term. The duel with Hamilton, however, ruined Burr's political career. In later years, Burr suffered from multiple strokes that left him partially paralyzed. He died in 1836 at the age of 80, nearly a forgotten man.

The US Capitol, 1858, before the renovations during the Civil War.

CAPITOL AND CAPITAL
Congress Comes of Age

It was like the first day of school. On January 3, 2013, a bright, sky blue afternoon, remarkably warm for a winter in the US capital, Washington, DC, the first-year class of the 113th Congress stood for their group photograph. Gathered on the steps of the Capitol Building, 82 new House members and 12 new senators beamed as the congressional photographer snapped away to record the historic event. And momentous it was, for the 113th Congress would be the most diverse in congressional history.

Of the new group, ready to serve as the people's delegates, 24 were women; four, African American; five, Asian American; and 10, Latino. There was Representative Tulsi Gabbard (Democrat from Hawaii), the first Hindu to serve in Congress. Mazie Hirono (Democrat from Hawaii) would be the first Buddhist senator. Representative Kyrsten Sinema (Democrat from Arizona) was the first openly bisexual congresswoman. Wisconsin's Tammy Baldwin is the first declared gay politician elected to the US Senate. With the 113th Congress, white males no longer made up the majority of House Democrats.

The average age of the newcomers copied the Congress as a whole. In the House, the freshmen class averaged 58 years old. In the Senate, it was slightly higher, at 61. Of note, Tammy Duckworth would begin her term as a Democratic representative from Illinois. A double-amputee veteran of the Iraq War, she is, not surprisingly, a strong advocate for equal rights for military women.

Alan Lowenthal, a House Democrat from California, was born in 1941. When asked about his game plan, he responded, "Job creation and renewable energy." Harry Hamburg, a new senator from Maine, is an independent, born in 1944, with **bipartisanship** (cooperation between political parties) being his aim. Ann Wagner, a House Republican from Montana, was born in 1962. Economic growth is her biggest concern. House member Brad Wenstrup, a Republican from Ohio, born in 1958, hopes to make health care a central focus. Deb Fisher, a new Republican senator from Nebraska, born in 1951, wants to reduce the size of the federal government. And Elizabeth Warren, a Democratic senator from Massachusetts, born in 1949, hopes to rebuild the middle class.

While most members of the freshmen class had at least visited Washington, DC, before being elected, they were no doubt given the grand tour of both the capitol and the capital, once the photographic session was over. It is also certain that the new representatives and senators were awed by what they saw.

The US Capitol Building, the home of Congress, the legislative branch of the federal government, stands on what was formerly known as Jenkins Hill, a plateau rising 88 feet above the nearby Potomac River. Now known as Capitol Hill, the area was named after the Capitoline Hill of the ancient Roman Republic.

The Capitol itself has undergone many modifications and expansions since its construction began in 1800. Today, the centerpiece under the massive dome erected during the Civil War (1860–1865) is the great Rotunda. In 1865, the Italian painter Constantino Brumidi, the "Michelangelo of the Capitol," painted a huge fresco under the dome. Depicting the *Apotheosis* [glorification] *of George Washington*, it is 180 feet above the Rotunda floor.

North of the Rotunda, on the second floor of the Capitol Building, is the Senate chamber, where 100 US senators preside. South of the Rotunda, also on the second floor, is the **House chamber**, large enough to accommodate the 435 members of the House of Representatives. Surrounding the Capitol Building, but still part of what is called Capitol Hill, are structures to accommodate the Supreme Court and the **Library of Congress**, as well as huge office buildings for members of Congress and their staff. The freshman members of Congress must have been impressed and humbled by what they experienced.

Congressional Cup and Saucer

ALL GOVERNMENTS, from dictatorships to democracies, are required to carry out three main functions. They must make laws, execute laws, and judge, or interpret, the laws. The United States, being a democracy, chose to structure its government into three separate branches, which, while working together and at the same time checking each other, conduct the above functions. There would be a legislative branch to make the laws, an executive branch to carry out the laws, and a judicial branch to interpret the laws.

The legislative branch is called the Congress. The word is derived from Latin for "coming together." The Congress consists of two chambers. One chamber is the Senate. There are two senators from every state, regardless of its size. Thus, today the Congress has 100 senators. The House of Representatives has 435 members who are often called, confusingly, congressmen or congresswomen—period. They represent **districts** within a state. The number of representatives each state gets is determined by its population, with the more people, the more representatives. Even so, every state, no matter how small, is guaranteed at least one representative.

★ **CHECKS AND BALANCES** ★

"If men were angels, no government would be necessary," wrote James Madison, a founding father. "If angels were to govern men, neither external nor internal controls on government would be necessary. In framing a government which is to be administered by men over men, the great difficulty is this: You must first enable the government to control the governed; and in the next place, oblige it to control itself."

In establishing such a government, the framers of the Constitution divided governing powers among three branches: the legislative, executive, and judicial. Each branch was to provide a check and balance on the ambition of the others. Yet the actual division of power was not clear-cut. The Constitution never constructed walls between the three branches. The Constitution implies many overlapping powers, which each of the branches have claimed.

Presidents, for example, have often wanted to be the only ones to make foreign policy, with no interference from Congress. Congress, in turn, has frequently wished to define how its laws must be administered by the executive branch. And the courts, from time to time, have tended to overreach by interpreting legislation in ways that Congress never intended.

Thus, while our government is structured on a separation of powers, woven into that separation are overlapping **checks and balances**. This system of checks and balances requires Congress and the president to work together if anything is to be accomplished.

The separation of powers, where checks and balance occur, can often result in a slow, inefficient, and even deadlocked government. Yet, as Supreme Court Justice Louis D. Brandeis pointed out in 1926, the principle "was adopted by the Constitution of 1787, not to promote efficiency" but to keep any one branch from exercising too much power.

Create Your Own "Congressional Money"

CONGRESS IS the branch of our government charged with coining money and regulating its value (Article I, Section 8). In this activity, you will create your own "Congressional Money."

Materials

★ 4 sheets light-colored construction paper, 9 × 12 inches

★ Access to a photocopier

★ Scissors

★ A few sheets of white paper, 8½ × 11 inches

★ Pencil

★ Colored pencils or pens

★ Glue stick

★ Ruler

1. Choose a sheet of colored paper that you will use to make dollar bills. From this sheet you will make eight, $1 bills. Hold the sheet lengthwise and fold it in half. Cut along the fold. Take one of the half-sheets and fold it widthwise to create four folds. Cut along the fold lines. You now have four "dollar bills," each 2¼ inches wide (9 inches divided by four) and 6 inches long (12 inches divided by two). Repeat for the other half-sheet. Set your eight $1 bill sheets aside.

2. Photocopy the two ovals shown in this exercise onto a sheet of white paper. Into the small oval, draw an outline portrait of a member of Congress who you think is of historical note. In the large oval make a simple line drawing of an illustration that depicts a major event in that congressperson's life. Keep your drawings simple because you will be using your colored pencils to highlight them.

3. Make eight photocopies of both the small and large ovals you have just illustrated.

4. Color in each oval as you wish. Make all the small ovals the same and all the large ovals the same.

5. Cut out all 16 ovals.

6. Apply a glue stick to the back of one of the small ovals. On what will be the front of your dollar bill, place the small oval in the center, with the long diameter in a vertical position. (Use a ruler to find the center.) Apply a glue stick to one of the large ovals, placing it on the back of your dollar bill, with the long diameter centered in the horizontal position. (Use a ruler to find the center.) Repeat for the remaining dollar bills.

7. Add a number "1" on the four corners of each dollar bill, on both sides.

8. Write the last name of your congressperson at the bottom of the small oval, curving the letters around the bottom. With the large oval, do something similar, but with a name identifying the illustration depicted.

9. Follow the above eight steps for the $5, $10, and $20 bills.

10. You can now use your "Congressional Money" to "purchase" small items from fellow students. They, of course, can do the same with their money.

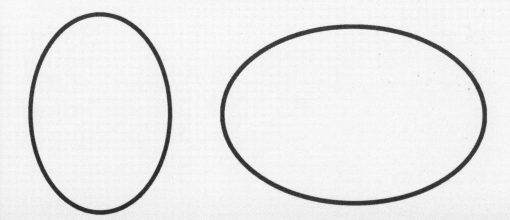

Congresses are established every two years and are thus numbered. The First Congress met from March 4, 1789, to March 4, 1791. The 100th Congress met from January 3, 1987, to January 3, 1989. Each Congress, in turn, meets for two sessions. Each session lasts close to a year.

The executive branch is led by the president of the United States. The president is elected by the entire country and serves a four-year term. The president's job, carried out through employees of the federal government, is to enforce the laws.

The judicial branch is headed by a Supreme Court, consisting of nine justices. The Supreme Court interprets the laws according to the Constitution.

The US Congress is a bicameral (from the Latin *bi*, meaning "two," and *camera*, meaning "chamber") institution. Thus, it consists of two separate bodies that share legislative duties. Both chambers of Congress, the House and the Senate, must pass bills in exactly the same form for them to eventually become law.

Though the three branches of government are supposedly coequal, it is clear that the Constitution intends that the legislative branch, the Congress, be supreme. After all, it is the Congress that is empowered to define the structure and duties of the other two branches.

The House of Representatives was meant by our framers to be the most representative ele-ment in the government. Members are directly elected by the people for two-year terms. Of the more than 10,000 representatives who have served in Congress over its 200-plus years, not a single one was ever appointed to the office. All have been elected. Being chosen every two years, it was hoped that members of the House would not stray too far from popular opinion. As founding father James Madison explained, "The House should have an immediate dependence on, and an intimate sympathy with, the people."

Surrender of British forces after the Battle of Yorktown, ending the Revolutionary War.
Library of Congress LC-DIG-pga-1668

The Senate was, as originally established, one step removed from popular voting. Senators were selected by their state legislatures. They were compared to ambassadors, representing their state's political establishment in Congress. Today, as a result of the 17th Amendment to the Constitution (passed in 1913), senators are, like representatives, directly elected by the people. Senators, however, serve six-year terms, thus allowing them, it is hoped, to temper sudden and violent popular passions expressed in the House. (Senators are divided into three classes, with one class, or one-third of the Senate, standing for election every two years.)

Thomas Jefferson, primary author of the Declaration of Independence, supposedly asked George Washington why a Senate was necessary. Washington responded with the question, "Why did you pour that coffee into your saucer?"

"To cool it," Jefferson replied.

"Even so," said Washington, "we pour legislation into the senatorial saucer to cool it."

Two Chambers—One Congress

While the 1787 Philadelphia Convention met to draft a new Constitution, which would define the Congress, the members agreed to a bicameral legislature, but there was vigorous debate as to the type of representation each chamber would reflect. In what became known as the Great Compromise, it was decided that one chamber (the House) would provide proportional representation, whereas the other chamber (the Senate) would provide equal representation. Thus, the large states got what they wanted, a chamber (the House) based on population that clearly gave them an advantage. The smaller states, however, were assured that no matter how few people they had, all states would have two members in the other chamber (the Senate). It was a compromise.

The Constitution requires that a census, or head count, of individuals residing in the United States be taken every 10 years. Based on the results, states are assigned a certain number of congressional districts, where in each district one representative is elected by the citizens living in that district. Originally, when the country was young, there was one representative for every 30,000 people. Today, with a national population of 312 million, and 435 House seats, a congressional district averages about 710,000 individuals.

As the young country grew in population, more House seats were created. Finally, in 1911, to keep the House at a manageable size, it was decided to cap, or freeze, the number of representatives at 435. Thus, because the size of the House is now fixed, as the nation's numbers increase, one state's gain means another state's loss. Still, even though a state with a population of less than 710,000 will get one House seat, the House of Representatives is judged to be well apportioned (divided up).

Not so in the Senate. The US Senate is considered to be one of the most malapportioned (unsuitably apportioned) legislatures in the democratic world. This is so because small states get the same number of senators as do large ones. As one scholar has noted, "The nine largest states are home to 51 percent of the population but elect only 18 percent of the Senate; the 26 smallest states control 52 percent of the Senate but hold only 18 percent of the population." Today, the spread between California, the most populous state, and Wyoming, the least populous state, is 53 to 1.

In terms of leadership, in the US Senate the vice president of the United States is the Senate president. In the vice president's absence, the **president pro tempore** (pro tempore is Latin, meaning "for the time being") is the presiding officer. Typically, the president pro tempore is the most senior member of the majority party.

The Senate also elects majority and minority political party (Democratic and Republican) leaders. The Senate **majority leader** plays a large role in determining the chamber's agenda and the leadership of **committees**.

Then there are Senate **majority** and **minority whips**. These whips are "party people," serving as deputies to their party leaders. They work to ensure party solidarity when it comes time to vote on legislation.

The House is led by the Speaker of the House, a representative who is a member of the majority

An idyllic Washington before it became a federal city. Library of Congress LC-DIG-ppmsca-15714

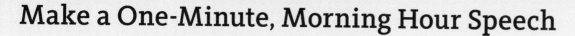

Make a One-Minute, Morning Hour Speech

AT THE BEGINNING of a new **legislative day**, both houses of Congress have what is known as the **morning hour**. In the House, this is a time when any member can speak on any subject for one minute. A representative usually does this to get his or her comments in the *Congressional Record*. In this activity, you will be giving a one-minute speech in front of your class, on any subject you like.

Materials
★ 1 note card, 3 × 5 inches
★ Pen or pencil

1. In deciding what to talk about, you might first want to select a category, such as family, school, community, nation, or world. If you choose family, for example, here are some topics that might get you thinking: skateboarding, cars, travel, growing vegetables, books, heroes, memories, new toys, awards, colors, food, sports, dreams, holidays, hobbies, planes, art, houses, new video games, movies, brothers and sisters—the list is endless.

2. Keep in mind, a one-minute speech is short—very short. Nonetheless, your speech should tell a story, one that has a beginning, a middle, and an end.

3. When speaking in front of the class, stand up straight and speak in a loud, crisp, pleasant, optimistic, and controlled voice. Make eye contact with your audience; try not to look down at your feet. Above all, show enthusiasm. Enthusiasm is contagious; you want your audience to feel your excitement.

4. It is always good to inject as much humor into your speech as possible, even if it is a sad subject. However, it is not necessary to make your speech into a one-minute joke. If your speech is on a personal topic, any mistakes or goofs you encountered in what you did will usually result in classroom laughter. Smile as much as possible; laugh along with the class.

5. Practice your speech in the days before you are assigned to deliver it. If you want, make a few notes on a note card. Write down only the main points. Practice reciting your speech. You can do this almost anywhere: going to or from school, in a car, while waiting in line, or when you get out of school early. A great place to practice is in the bath or shower.

6. As you come to the end of your speech in class, say "thank you" and walk off the "stage." You are now on your way to doing what members of Congress do almost every day—speak!

political party. Basically, the Speaker administers the proceedings on the House floor (where speaking, negotiating, and voting take place).

When it comes to the floor, however, each party elects a floor leader, known as the House majority leader and the House **minority leader**. The majority leader is second in command to the Speaker, and the minority leader is the head of his/her party.

The House of Representatives also has party whips who function as they do in the Senate.

To be elected to the House, one must be at least 25 years of age, a citizen of the United States for at least seven years, and a legal resident of the state that elects him or her. To become a US senator, a person must be at least 30 years of age, a US citizen for the past nine years, and a legal resident of the state that elects him or her. Needless to say, the 94 freshmen members of the 113th Congress met the qualification to serve.

The First Congress

THE FIRST Congress, meeting in March 1789, did not convene in Washington, DC. There was practically nothing there at the time. Rather, both the Senate and the House gathered in Federal Hall, a building at the corner of Wall and Nassau Streets, in New York City. It would be almost a dozen years, with a side stay in Philadelphia, before Congress's permanent home in Washington would be ready.

In Federal Hall, the House chamber was located on the first floor. The Senate took up residency on the floor above the House. It is for this reason that from then on the House of Representatives would often be known as the Lower House while the Senate would be referred to as the Upper House. Identifying both chambers as such had everything to do with architecture and nothing to do with the supposed superiority of the Senate over the House of Representatives.

Of the 59 representatives who were elected to serve in the House, only 13 showed up on March 4, the day the first session of the First Congress was to begin. The missing members were delayed by roads deep in mud, riddled with potholes, or washed away by floodwaters. It wasn't until April Fool's Day, of all days, that the House had the necessary 30 members to make a **quorum** (the minimum attendance—half the members plus one—necessary to conduct business).

Almost immediately, the House (but not the Senate) opened its doors to the public. However, according to historian Robert V. Remini, "Members regularly complained that the crowd in the gallery cracked nuts during the debates, much to their annoyance, and well-to-do visitors frequently found that

Know Your District

THERE ARE MANY sources of data about congressional districts. One in particular is the *Congressional District Demographic Profiles* by *Proximity* at http://proximityone.com/cdprofiles.htm. The website provides detailed data about the population of every congressional district. In this activity, you will learn more about your district and prepare a simple report and chart displaying your data.

Materials
★ Access to a computer with a printer
★ Calculator
★ Drawing compass
★ Protractor
★ Ruler
★ Set of different colored crayons or colored markers

1. Go to the Proximity website at http://proximityone.com/cdprofiles.htm. Click the "State" dropdown menu to view districts in a selected state. Find your district. (Refer to the information folder you assembled in the "Find Your Representative" activity.)

2. Select one of the four categories of data: (1) "Age, Gender, Race, Ethnic," (2) "Social," (3) "Economic," (4) "Housing." For example, you might choose "Economic."

3. Select a subcategory. Under "Economics" you might choose "Occupation." Note that for the latest year data is available, you are given both actual numbers and percentages. You will place this information in your report. Note, also, that the various groups under the subcategory give percentages that add up to 100 percent. In preparing your pie chart, you will need to determine how many degrees of each percentage given exists in a 360-degree circle. You do this by multiplying the percentage given by 360. For example, if 43 percent is given, multiply 0.43 (the decimal equivalent of 43 percent) times 360. You should come up with 155 degrees.

4. At the bottom of your report, draw a circle as large as possible. This will be the start of your pie graph. With a ruler, draw a light line through the center to the outer edges of the circle. This will be your reference line.

5. Use your protractor to mark off in degrees the values you calculated. For example, from the reference line, you would mark on the circumference of the circle 155 degrees (it doesn't matter what direction from the reference line). From the center of the circle, draw a line to the 155 degree mark on the circle's circumference. The space be-

continued…

Know Your District—*continued*

tween the reference line and the line you just drew is the area of the pie graph that represents 43 percent.

6. Complete divisions for the pie graph (don't worry if you are a bit off on the divisions). You may wish to color in the various divisions, each with a different color. If you do so, you will want to mark each group on your list with the color you used on your pie chart.

7. Write a one-page report summarizing your data. An example is shown here.

California, 26th District

Report

ECONOMIC DATA

Occupations

2009

By Linda Hernandez

This report shows the types of jobs people held in the 26th Congressional District in California in 2009. Six occupational groups are listed. For each group, the total number of individuals is given, along with their percentage of the total. Thus, there were 90,769 workers in sales and office jobs, which is 27.81 percent of the total workforce in the 26th Congressional District in California.

Occupation:	2009 Numbers:	2009 Percentage:
Civilian employed populations (those individuals not in the armed forces) 16 years and over	326,358	100.00
(1) Management, professional, and related jobs	140,338	43.00
(2) Service	48,543	14.87
(3) Sales and office	90,769	27.81
(4) Farming, fishing, and forestry	237	0.07
(5) Construction, extraction, maintenance, and repair	20,410	6.25
(6) Production, transportation, and material moving	26,061	7.99

Pie Chart of Various Types of Jobs

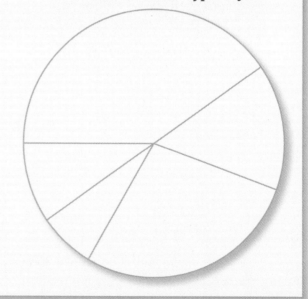

pickpockets had relieved them of their valuables, discarding empty wallets at the Battery [a military fort]."

Five days after the House began its work, the Senate, expecting 26 members, achieved a quorum. The First Congress of the United States was ready for business.

During the early Congresses, the turnover was high. Low pay was undoubtedly a factor. One of the first things members of the First Congress did was to fix their salary—at $6 a day during the session plus travel expenses. (Senators would get a dollar a day more until March 1796. Senate pay would equal that of representatives thereafter.)

Of course, the First Congress (March 4, 1789, to March 4, 1791) did far more than decide how much they and other federal officials would be paid. Indeed, the First Congress is considered to be the most productive ever. To be sure, they had so much more to do, being the first. This Congress would secure revenue, establish executive departments, create the judicial system, and enact the Bill of Rights. The members took their responsibilities seriously. It was a proper start.

★ ELIZABETH WARREN ★

When Elizabeth Warren, Democrat from Massachusetts, assumed her duties as a newly elected US senator on January 3, 2013, she came to the job with quite a resume. Born in 1949, Warren received a bachelor of science degree in 1970 and a law degree in 1976. She was an elementary school speech pathologist, a law professor, a bankruptcy expert, and is the author of nine books, including the bestselling *The Two-Income Trap*. Dr. Warren was also the chair of the Congressional Oversight Panel for the Troubled Asset Relief Program (2008–2010). She is considered an expert on consumer financial protection.

Senator Elizabeth Warren was elected to the US Senate in 2012.
Courtesy of Senator Elizabeth Warren

Warren, firmly in the liberal camp, is not afraid to take on anyone, including fellow Democrats. In an exchange with Senator Joe Manchin, a Democrat from West Virginia, regarding student loan legislation, she said, "They're already making money off the backs of students, and this adds another $1 billion." Manchin, downplaying the exchange, responded, "I love her, she is a dear friend. We've never had one cross word since she's been here, and we agree 90 percent of the time."

Liberal as Senator Warren is, she recognizes that getting anything done in the Senate requires compromise. Responding to the passage of compromise legislation on the student loan issue, she said, "They've done a wonderful job, Democrats and Republicans. I admire what they've done. Is it what I want? I'd rather have something a little different, but I'm going to take this because that's what we do. We're legislators. We compromise."

★ ★

Men and women in the gallery of the Senate during the impeachment trial of Andrew Johnson. Library of Congress LC-cph-3c19581

HIGH CRIMES AND MISDEMEANORS
Congress and Impeachment

On May 16, 1868, the US Senate sitting in judgment of President Andrew Johnson voted 35 to 19 to remove him from office. Since it took two-thirds of those senators present to convict Johnson on **impeachment** charges brought by the House of Representatives, 35 votes were not enough. Senators hoping to depose Johnson needed 36 votes. They never got them. Seven Republican senators, defying their party's leadership, voted (along with 12 Democrats) to acquit (clear) the president. Their action saved not only President Andrew Johnson but possibly the institution of the presidency.

The US Constitution (Article II, Section 4) gives the Congress the power to impeach and remove "The President, Vice President, and all civil Officers of the United States" for serious violation of the public trust: treason, bribery, or other high crimes and misdemeanors. Doing so involves a two-step process.

First, the House of Representatives votes to impeach, that is, formally charge, as with an indictment (accusation) in a court of law. The majority of House members must vote for the charges in order to impeach a president.

Second, the Senate then sits as a court. Its job is to determine guilt or innocence. If at least two-thirds of the Senate votes to convict the president on any of the impeachment charges, the president is guilty, and the chief executive of the United States will be removed from office. The Senate may then, by a simple majority, choose to forbid the now former president from ever holding public office again. The verdict in an impeachment trial is final—there is no appeal.

In determining what impeachment meant, the framers of the Constitution struggled over one key issue above all else: what does "high crimes and misdemeanors mean"? Treason is defined in the Constitution; bribery is defined by law; but exactly what is meant by "high crimes and misdemeanors"? The authors of the Constitution were purposely vague on the subject. They wanted to use impeachment as a "powerful legislative check upon executive and judicial wrongdoing."

In the end, the impeachment process sought to achieve two goals. One goal was a full public inquiry into charges of wrongdoing by a federal official. Placing the responsibility for this action in the House of Representatives would, it was felt, accomplish that objective. And, two, if articles of impeachment were voted on by the House, a public trial would take place in the Senate. If a president of the United States is being tried, the Constitution specifies that the chief justice of the Supreme Court shall preside over the Senate trial.

President Andrew Johnson is served an impeachment summons from the US House of Representatives. Library of Congress LC-cph 3c6849

Still, over more than 200 years of our history and 17 impeachment cases, a key question remains as to just how political the whole process is. The framers sincerely hoped impeachment would not be used as a political weapon. Yet, in 1970, then Representative Gerald Ford declared: "An impeachable offense is whatever a majority of the House of Representatives considers it to be at a given moment in history." There is no question that politics would play a strong part when the first president of the United States to be impeached, Andrew Johnson, stood against his congressional foes.

The Tenure of Office Act

In 1821, at the age of 13, Andrew Johnson, the man who would become the 17th president of the United States, was illiterate—he could not read a word. Growing up in the rural poverty of North Carolina, Johnson had received no formal schooling whatsoever. Yet, by his force of personality and ambition, and with the help of a kindly foreman at the tailor shop where he was apprenticed, Johnson learned to read by the time he was 15. It wasn't until Johnson was over 20 that his wife taught him to write.

As determined and dedicated as Johnson was, he was a stubborn man. Having almost no formal education, he saw issues as simply right or wrong. Complicated problems frustrated Johnson. He could often let a personal insult pass without a second thought, but he could not yield a point. Instead, he would fight for his position with everything he had.

Johnson moved to Tennessee in the early 1820s and eventually entered politics. He rose rapidly, becoming mayor of Greeneville, state representative, congressman, governor of Tennessee, and US senator. Because Johnson was the only Southern senator to remain loyal to the Union, President Abraham Lincoln saw to it that Johnson became his vice president in 1865. When Lincoln was assassinated on April 14 of that year, Johnson became president of the United States.

Make a Capital for the Capitol

THERE ARE MANY columns with capitals (the uppermost part of a column) on Capitol Hill. In its simplest form, each column has a capital at the top, a base at the bottom, and a vertical element in between known as the shaft. Three major styles of capitals from ancient Greece are called Doric, Ionic, and Corinthian. The Corinthian capital is the most decorative. In this activity, you will construct and decorate a column that reflects what is important to your state.

Materials

* ★ Paper towel cardboard core, 1½ inch in diameter and 11 inches long
* ★ 2 yogurt cups that taper toward the opening (Yoplait yogurt cups are tapered and have just the right size opening for the towel core to fit into)
* ★ White glue
* ★ Acrylic paints, assorted colors, with brushes
* ★ Scissors
* ★ 1 sheet white paper, 8½ × 11 inches
* ★ Ruler
* ★ Pencil

1. Think about what defines or reflects your state. For example, a capital could use corn or another crop as its motif (repeated design) to show the importance of farming in your state. Or you may want to choose a state flower or a manufactured item. If you live in Michigan, for example, you might select the automobile as a design element.

2. Insert one end of the paper towel core into a yogurt cup. Make sure it goes to the bottom. Squirt a bead of glue around the rim where the two objects join. Let the glue dry.

3. Repeat the above procedure for the other yogurt cup. Choose which cup will be your column base and which one will be your column capital.

4. Paint the entire column, with its base and capital, white. Let it dry. You may have to apply a second coat.

5. Cut a white sheet of paper to 3 × 8 inches. This sheet will be used as a guide for what you will draw on the capital itself. Lay the sheet horizontally and with a pencil, mark off 1-inch divisions. Draw a light, vertical line at each point.

6. Using the vertical lines as a guide, sketch seven symbols representing products from your state. The symbols can be the same (like a stalk of corn) or each one can be different.

7. Fill in the areas surrounding the symbols you have drawn with related designs.

8. Using your sheet, mark 1-inch points on the upper rim of your capital. Draw eight vertical lines down the length of the capital.

9. Using the paper sheet as a guide, with a pencil reproduce your artwork onto the capital.

10. Using assorted paint colors, paint in your artwork.

11. If you choose, decorate the base, perhaps with horizontal bands of color.

12. Share your capital and column with others. Compare your design and artwork.

Capital

Shaft

Base

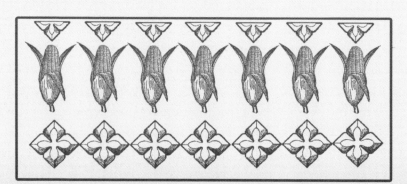

With the Civil War at an end, the historical period known as Congressional Reconstruction began, an interval that lasted until 1877. Johnson favored what he thought were Lincoln's wishes, a quick and lenient return of the South into the Union. On the other hand, a group of Radical Republicans in Congress, led by Representative Thaddeus Stevens, argued that the 11 former Confederate states, having seceded from the Union, had committed "state suicide" and were now conquered territories. They would be admitted back into the Union only if they ensured the civil rights and liberties of the freedmen (former slaves).

Johnson did not favor what he felt was this too drastic approach. He **vetoed** the Freedmen's Bureau Bill, which, among other things, provided funds to construct schools for the freed slaves. Though Congress overrode Johnson's veto of the bill, the battle lines were drawn. The Radical Republicans in Congress sought a way to remove Johnson from office. With their passage of the Tenure of Office Act in 1867 (over Johnson's veto), they believed they had found a means to do so.

The Constitution makes it clear that the Senate is required to provide **advice and consent** to major executive branch nominations. The document, however, says nothing about how such officials might be removed, other than through impeachment. Radical Republicans in

Congress now sought to require Johnson to seek approval before he could *remove* any cabinet officer or other high-ranking official. The Tenure of Office Act was designed to prevent Johnson from firing such officials without Congress's approval. Johnson felt the act was unconstitutional. Ignoring it, in 1868 he fired Secretary of War Edwin Stanton without consulting Congress.

Stanton supported a tough Reconstruction policy. By discharging his secretary of war, Johnson signaled his intent to replace Stanton

Thaddeus Stevens tries to rally support for the ouster of President Andrew Johnson.
Library of Congress LC-cph 3c6848

29

★ THADDEUS STEVENS ★

In his final months, Representative Thaddeus Stevens of Pennsylvania was so feeble and weak in the heart that he had to be carried into the House chamber on a chair by two strong colleagues. Yet he remained active until his death on August 11, 1868, having fought to abolish slavery and to draft the 14th Amendment during Reconstruction. Known as a leader of the Radical Republicans, Stevens took aim at President Johnson, leading the cause to impeach the president. As chairman of the powerful Ways and Means Committee, Stevens used his influence to block Johnson from readmitting former Confederate states into the Union until they agreed to provide full equality for former slaves.

Post–Civil War Southerners despised Stevens. They saw him as a vindictive, fanatical, out-of-control legislator determined to punish the South. Southerners believed that Stevens supported voting rights for blacks only to secure their votes for the Republican Party. On the other hand, many Northerners, and virtually all freedmen, worshiped Representative Stevens as the defender of the belief, enshrined in the Declaration of Independence, that all people are created equal.

Nearing death, in the summer of 1868, Stevens requested burial in the Shreiner-Concord Cemetery in Lancaster, Pennsylvania, because the state accepted all races. Stevens composed his own epitaph (funeral oration), which read, "I repose in this quiet and secluded spot, not for any natural preference for solitude. But finding other cemeteries limited as to race by charter rules, I have chosen this that I might illustrate in my death the principles which I advocated through a long life, equality of man before his creator."

Though ill and physically disabled, Thaddeus Stevens fought the good fight as he saw it, to his end.

Library of Congress LC-cph 3a17688

with an officer more in keeping with a less radical approach in dealing with the post–Civil War South. After President Johnson violated the Tenure of Office Act by dismissing Stanton, the Radical Republicans now sought to remove the president himself—by impeaching him.

Radical Republicans Miss by One

ON FEBRUARY 24, 1868, three days after President Johnson dismissed Edwin Stanton, the House of Representatives, in a vote of 126 to 47, passed a resolution to impeach the president for high crimes and misdemeanors. It was the first time in the nation's history that a president had ever been impeached. One week later, the House adopted 11 articles of impeachment against the chief executive. Nine of the articles focused on the president's dismissal of Stanton. The 11th article scolded him for resisting Congress and was, in many respects, a summation of the first 10.

The trial began in the Senate, with the chief justice of the Supreme Court, Salmon P. Chase, presiding. Committees were organized to represent the prosecution and the defense. Eight Republicans were selected as prosecutors, to argue for conviction. Three Republicans and two Democrats made up the defense team.

There was much haggling over procedures, and, as a result, the trial was delayed for over a month. On March 30, 1868, the proceedings officially began.

The prosecution, not surprisingly, concentrated on Johnson's violation of the Tenure of Office Act. To the eight Republicans searching for conviction, it seemed a cut-and-dried case—Johnson had violated the law. The defense said not so fast. They argued that Johnson had not violated the Tenure of Office Act because the act did not apply to him. According to Johnson's supporters, President Lincoln did not reappoint Stanton as secretary of war at the start of his second term in March 1865. Therefore, Stanton was a leftover appointment from the 1860 cabinet. Thus the secretary was removed from protection by the Tenure of Office Act.

While the Radical Republicans hoped that all Republican senators would vote to convict the president, they knew there were senators in their party who were wavering. Indeed, seven Republicans braved intense pressure and threats to their political careers to hold back on a vote for conviction. One in particular, Senator Edmund G. Ross of Kansas, took the full brunt of the attack. The *New York Tribune* reported that

Edmund Ross in particular was "mercilessly dragged this way and that by both sides, hunted like a fox night and day and badgered

Track a Bill through Congress

GOVTRACK is a website that enables users to track the status of any bill in Congress. Its purpose is to help educate voters about the legislative process. In this activity, you use GovTrack to keep track of the status of three bills of your choice. One of the most interesting aspects of GovTrack is its ability to predict the chances of a particular bill making it out of committee and being enacted by the Congress.

Materials

★ Access to a computer with a printer
★ Paper and pen or pencil

1. Go to the GovTrack home page at www.GovTrack.us. Select: "Bills & Resolutions" under "find Information."

2. Select: "By Subject."

3. Under "Browse Bills by Subject," make your choice. Note that bills are listed as either Senate Bills (S.xxx), House Bills (H.R.xxx), joint Senate/House Bills (S.J.Res.xxx), or Senate simple resolutions (S.Res.xxx).

4. Select a bill that interests you. Note the bill's number, complete name, sponsor, status, and progress.

5. Note the bill's prognosis (prospect of passing). If the bill is not yet out of committee, two

percentages are given: (1) chance of getting past committee; (2) chance of being enacted. If the bill is already out of committee, the chances of it passing the full chamber are given. Compare the percentage(s) given with those for the previous Congress.

6. Select "Summary: Library of Congress." Read the summary and make notes, then return to the previous page.

7. Select "Cosponsors." Note the number of Democrats and Republicans.

8. Select "Committees." If there is more than one committee listed, select any one. Under the committee you have chosen, note the following:

> Chairman
> Ranking Member
> Number of Republicans
> Number of Democrats

9. Go to the committee's website and look it over. Note any points of interest.

10. Close the website to return to GovTrack. Repeat the above process for a second, then a third bill. On three separate sheets of paper, document your findings for each bill. Compare your three bills, noting in particular which one has the best and which one has the worst chance of becoming a law.

by his own Army and now trampled by the others." His background and life were investigated from top to bottom, and his constituents and colleagues pursued him throughout Washington to gain some inkling of his opinion.

On May 16, the Senate finally voted. It first passed judgment on Article 11. The Senate acquitted the president when the vote came down at 35 guilty and 19 not guilty. The prosecution fell one vote short of the 36 needed to convict. There were two more votes taken on two additional articles, but the outcome was the same. Soon after, anti-Johnson forces abandoned their efforts to remove the president. Not one of the seven Republicans who voted for acquittal was ever reelected to the Senate.

The Senate acting as a court of justice during the first impeachment trial of a president of the United States, that of Andrew Johnson.
Library of Congress LC-cph 3a5488

Historians have identified at least three factors leading to the Senate vote to acquit Johnson. One, if Johnson were removed, the Senate president pro tem, Benjamin Wade, would become president of the United States. He was simply too radical even for most Radical Republicans. Two, Johnson quietly agreed to cooperate with willing Republicans on future Reconstruction efforts. And, three, Ulysses S. Grant, a Civil War hero, had just been nominated as the Republican candidate for president. In his acceptance speech the General preached a return to peace.

Impeachment and Denial

ON DECEMBER 19, 1998, President Bill Clinton became the first elected president to be impeached by the House of Representatives. (Andrew Johnson was elected vice president and inherited the presidency upon the assassination of President Lincoln.) Though the House Judiciary Committee presented four articles of impeachment to the full House, only two were approved by the entire body. The 42nd president of the United States was charged with (1) perjury (lying under oath) and (2) obstruction of justice. Both claims stemmed from the Monica Lewinsky scandal. The entire impeachment and trial proceedings were considered by many to be highly **partisan** (adhering strictly to one's political party), bringing into question just how objective any impeachment of a president can be.

The allegations arose from a probe conducted by Kenneth Starr, a lawyer appointed to investigate a failed Arkansas land deal, known as Whitewater, that both Clinton and his wife, Hillary, were involved in. Soon the investigation broadened to include alleged abuses during Clinton's presidency, such as the firing of White House travel agents and misuse of FBI files. In the course of the inquiry, Linda Tripp (a former White House secretary) provided Starr with taped phone conversations between her and a former White House intern named Monica Lewinsky. In those conversations, Lewinsky discussed having an affair with the president.

In later testimony before a grand jury, Clinton denied he had ever had intimate relations with Lewinsky. Clinton issued similar denials to his cabinet, his staff, his family, and to members of Congress.

Over the next few weeks it became clear that Clinton's denial statements were false. On August 27, 1998, in a nationally televised address, Clinton admitted that he had engaged in an in-appropriate relationship with Lewinsky. However, the president strongly asserted that he had done nothing illegal.

Starr, in reporting to the House of Representatives, suggested that the president could have committed two impeachable offenses: perjury and obstruction of justice. Eventually, it was these two charges that led to the articles of impeachment that Clinton would face in a Senate trial.

That trial began on January 14, 1999. The prosecuting team took three days to present its case. Following that, the defense took the same amount of time to defend the president.

When it came time for a vote, the article alleging perjury failed on a 45 to 55 vote. The obstruction of justice article failed on a 50 to 50 vote. In both cases, 67 votes, constituting two-thirds of the 100-member Senate, would have been needed to convict.

Curiously, throughout the entire impeachment proceedings, President Clinton's public approval ratings climbed steadily, at one point reaching 70 percent. Yet there is little question that the embarrassing personal revelations that fed the impeachment efforts tainted Clinton, and by extension, the presidency itself.

✶ ✶

A group of activists at the National American Woman Suffrage Association parade held in Washington, DC, March 3, 1913. Library of Congress LC-DIG-ggbain-114

A NEW AGE DAWNING
Congress and the Progressive Era

In the era after the Civil War, from 1865 through the 1920s, America changed in monumental ways. Industrialization, fed by expanded railroading, rapidly advanced, particularly in the North. The concentration of super rich barons of industry gave the term Gilded Age to the late 1800s, though most urban poor people lived in squalid poverty. Internationally, the nation chose expansion, in effect becoming an empire. In the Pacific, the Philippines, Guam, and the Hawaiian islands came under American control. So, too, did the islands of Cuba and Puerto Rico in the Caribbean. The United States was growing stronger and more powerful; it was becoming a force commanding recognition, respect, and for some, fear, throughout the world.

Congress, reflecting the times, underwent historic change. One particular individual, who would become Speaker of the House, revolutionized the way the lower chamber conducted business. Thomas B. Reed, of Maine, soon to be known as "Czar Reed" for his dictatorial rule, altered forever the power relationships between majority and minority parties in the House of Representatives. That change affected not only Congress but also the society it sought to govern.

When Reed was elected Speaker, at the start of the 51st Congress in 1889, he was a man standing six feet, three inches tall and weighing over 250 pounds (some said over 300 pounds). According to one account:

> He [Reed] was one of the few men in public life at whom strangers on the street turned to stare. He had a massive two-story head, thatched with thin, flossy hair, a scant mustache, and a lily-white complexion. . . . Quick witted, ferociously intelligent and sharp tongued, he loved to deflate windbags with a stinging retort. To a fellow Republican he once remarked, "You are too big a fool to lead and you haven't got sense enough to follow."

At the time Reed took control of the House, the chamber's rules made it easy to block the passage of laws that one disagreed with. One tactic used to impede was known as the "disappearing quorum." To achieve a quorum (the minimum number of representatives required to conduct business), the House rules required that a majority of its members be present during

a vote in the chamber. At the time of the 51st Congress (1889–1891), a quorum required 166 representatives. Up until that period, if a member was present, but remained silent during roll call, he was not counted. The Democrats took full advantage of this "disappearing quorum" ploy to remain quiet when their names were read. In doing so, House business could not proceed, which often suited the Democrats just fine.

On January 29, 1890, in an issue regarding a disputed election in West Virginia, Reed, acting as Speaker, ordered the clerk of the House to record as present any member who was physically in the chamber but who did not respond during a **roll call vote**. Reed proceeded to announce the names of the silent members.

The House immediately broke into what one historian called "a deafening mass of individuals yelling, laughing, clapping, pounding their desks and stamping on the floor." Democrats were outraged. "For some minutes there was pandemonium with a hundred men in front of the Speaker's desk, shaking their fists at the man in the chair . . . and drowning one another's voice in their defiance."

Democratic Representative James B. Mc-Creary, of Kentucky, shouted, "I deny your right, Mr. Speaker, to count me as present, and I desire to read from the parliamentary law on the subject." Responding, Reed declared, "The Chair is making a statement of the fact that the

Speaker Reed destroys the disappearing quorum of House members who do not wish to be counted.
Library of Congress LC-cph 3b2237

gentleman from Kentucky is present. Does he deny it?"

In the coming days, some Democratic members took to hiding under their desks in hopes of not being detected.

Direct Election of Senators: The 17th Amendment

THE PROGRESSIVE Era, a period of social activism and political reform that took full form in the first two decades of the 20th century, saw the enactment of four constitutional amendments. The 16th Amendment created the federal income tax. The 17th Amendment provided for the direct election of senators. The 18th Amendment began the era of Prohibition, when the sale of liquor was forbidden throughout the United States. (The amendment was repealed, however, with the passage of the 21st Amendment.) Finally, the 19th Amendment gave women the right to vote. In this chapter, we will examine the 17th and 19th Amendments in some detail, starting with the 17th.

There are two ways the US Constitution can be amended. One, a bill to amend the Constitution must pass both the House and Senate by a two-thirds majority in each chamber. Once that happens, the bill goes to the states. At least three-quarters of the states must **ratify** (approve) the bill. If that takes place, the amendment be-

comes part of the Constitution. The only way the Constitution has ever been amended is by this method.

There is a second way to amend the Constitution, however. It has never been done,

---

★ THE SPEAKER OF THE HOUSE ★

The position of the Speaker of the House of Representatives is created in Article I, Section 2, Clause 5 of the US Constitution. The document reads, "The House of Representatives shall chuse [choose] their Speaker and other Officers; . . . "

The Speaker of the House, who is elected by the majority of House representatives, is the highest-ranking member in the lower chamber. The Speaker also stands second only to the vice president of the United States in line of presidential succession. Here are a few House facts about the Speaker:

★ **The first Speaker of the House:** Frederick A. C. Muhlenberg served from 1789 to 1791.
★ **The total number of Speakers:** To date, 53
★ **Longest-serving Speaker of the House:** Samuel Rayburn—17 years
★ **Shortest term of Speaker:** Theodore M. Pomeroy, on the closing day of the 40th

Congress in 1869. He was elected as a sign of respect from his colleagues.
★ **State with the most Speakers:** Massachusetts, with eight
★ **First (and only) Speaker to serve as president:** James K. Polk of Tennessee
★ **Longest election for Speaker:** After more than two months and 113 ballots, Nathaniel P. Banks was elected Speaker on February 2, 1856.
★ **First woman Speaker:** Nancy Pelosi of California became the first woman Speaker on January 4, 2007.
★ **Youngest Speaker elected:** Robert M. T. Hunter, elected on December 16, 1839, at the age of 30
★ **Oldest Speaker elected:** Henry T. Rainey, elected on March 9, 1933, at the age of 72
★ **First Speaker to approve regular TV feeds from the House chamber:** Thomas P. (Tip) O'Neill

Make a Federal Budget Pie Chart

EACH YEAR, the US Congress passes a federal budget that, after much negotiation with the executive branch, the president signs into law. For the fiscal year 2013, total spending equaled $3,685,000,000,000. In this activity, you will calculate the percentage of spending devoted to 10 budget categories and chart the results to show clearly how much government spends on each category.

Materials

* Access to a photocopier
* Pen or pencil
* Drawing compass
* Calculator
* Protractor
* Ruler
* 10 crayons or colored markers (each a different color)

1. Photocopy the data chart at right. Make sure the data chart is near the top of the sheet. Put your name on the sheet.

2. Calculate the percentage of federal spending for each category listed to the right. For example, to determine the percentage for pensions, divide the amount given in billions (874) by the total amount of the federal budget (3,685). The calculation is 874/3,685. You should get 0.24, or 24 percent. Fill in the rest of your data chart.

3. Calculate the number of degrees in a circle that each percentage represents. For example, 24 percent represents 86 degrees of a full (360-degree) circle. The calculation is 0.24 (the decimal equivalent of 24 percent) times 360. Fill in the rest of your data chart.

4. On your sheet of paper, draw a circle 6 inches in diameter. This will be the start of your pie graph. With a ruler, draw a light line through the center to the outer edges of the circle. This will be your reference line.

5. Use your protractor to mark off in degrees the values shown in your data chart. For example, from the reference line, mark on the circumference of the circle the 86-degree point. (It doesn't matter what direction from the reference line.) From the center of the circle, draw a line to the 86-degree mark on the circle's circumference. The space between the reference line and the line you just drew is the area of the pie graph devoted to "Pensions."

6. Complete divisions for the pie graph. (Don't worry if you are a bit off on the divisions.) Color in the various divisions, each with a different color.

7. Next to the spending category on your data chart, mark the color that corresponds to the one used on your pie chart.

8. You may want to present your chart to the entire class for discussion.

Data Chart			
Category	Spending in $ Billions	% of Total	Degrees on Pie Chart
Pensions	$874	24 percent	86 degrees
Health Care	$882		
Education	$98		
Defense	$857		
Welfare	$422		
Protection	$37		
Transportation	$94		
General Government	$56		
Other Spending	$141		
Interest	$222		
Total Spending	**$3,685**		

though it is provided for. If at least two-thirds of the legislatures of the states call for a Constitutional Convention, such a convention can propose one or more amendments. The amendments must then be sent to the states, where, if approved by three-fourths of the state legislatures, they become law. With this "state-led method" of amendment, neither the Congress nor the executive branch of government is involved.

One reason a Constitutional Convention has never been formed is the fear of a "runaway convention," where anything goes, where, conceivably, the whole Constitution is open to revision. No one seeking the passage of a particular amendment wants that.

Yet by 1912, the threat to form such a convention was real. Thirty-one states, one less than the two-thirds required to do so, had already taken action regarding a controversy that had reached a boiling point—direct election of US senators by popular vote.

The framers had written into the Constitution that senators would be chosen by state legislatures. Senators were to be seen as ambassadors from their states to the federal government. Such legislatures could, at least theoretically, instruct their senators to vote for or against various proposals. Furthermore, senators, more removed from the popular will of the people than representatives in the House, were thought

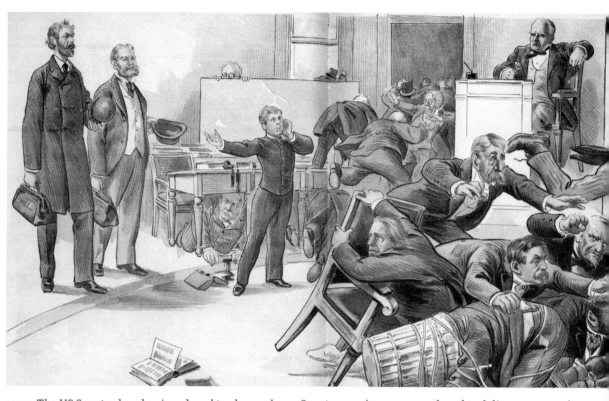

ABOVE: The US Senate chamber is reduced to chaos when a Senate page (a person employed to deliver messages) announces the unexpected arrival of "Investigators Lexow and Goff." Library of Congress LC-DIG-ppmsca-29117

LEFT: By the last decade of the 19th century, those favoring a prohibition on the sale of alcoholic beverages had grown in influence. Library of Congress LC-cph 3b741

capable of taking a more detached view on issues coming before Congress.

Over the years, reformers had tried to alter this senator appointment approach by getting Congress to pass an amendment allowing for the direct election of senators. In 1828, 1829, and 1855, serious proposals to do this were introduced in Congress. They went nowhere. By 1906, however, two concerns regarding the current system had taken center stage.

In that year, a popular novelist, David Graham Phillips, published a scathing attack on the Senate, accusing its members of the most open corruption. In a nine-part series in *Cosmopolitan*, Phillips, in what he titled "The Treason of the Senate," insisted that senators were tools of "the interests," corporations bent on having their way with Congress. "To be a senator," it was said, "was to be a suspect."

The Senate was seen by many as unrepresentative. It was, in the eyes of the press and other social critics, a "millionaires' club." Senators were highly partisan, while their integrity left a great deal to be desired.

Also, it was felt by many that legislative deadlock had become a serious problem. State legislatures had to agree on whom to appoint as senators. Some could not, and thus they delayed sending senators to Congress. In a few cases, states would, for a time, go without representation.

These criticisms could no longer be ignored. Something had to change. In the spirit of the Progressive Era, a proposal to **mandate** (require) direct elections of the Senate was finally introduced in the Congress on June 12, 1911. By 1913, the same year the 16th Amendment passed, so, too, did the 17th Amendment, providing for the direct election of US senators. From now on, though senators would serve as they always had, for six years, not two years as do representatives in the House, they would have to run for election by the people, just like their colleagues in the lower chamber.

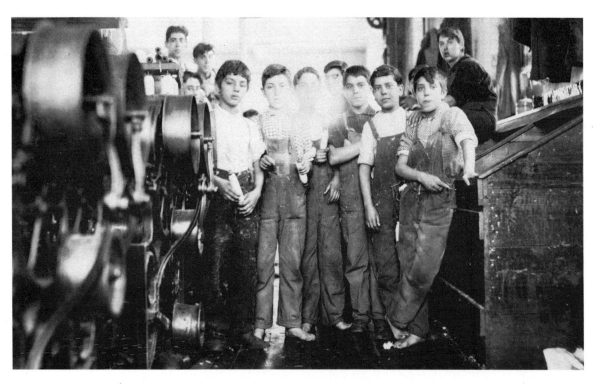

Child laborers in 1912, Fall River, Massachusetts, none of whom could read or write their own names.
Library of Congress LC-DIG-nclc-251

The effect was immediate. When the amendment passed, senators quickly learned to be more tuned in to public opinion in their state. Senators still received campaign money from special interests, of course. But it was the people who voted them into office. It was a far-reaching change in representative government.

A Woman's Right to Vote: The 19th Amendment

WOMEN PLAYED a critical part in passage of the 18th Amendment to prohibit the sale of intoxicating liquor. After all, it was largely their husbands who were drawn to drink, which, in too many cases, resulted in ruptured families and homes. The dedication and organizational skills acquired during the fight for Prohibition also found expression in a parallel effort to gain women the right to vote. That labor would end in passage of the 19th Amendment, in 1919, after decades of struggle.

In June 1917, as momentum for extending the suffrage (right to vote) to women gained ground, members of the National Woman's Party (NWP) picketed the White House. They were soon arrested. Many were thrown into prison at an abandoned workhouse in Occoquan, Virginia, and suffered horrible beatings at the hands of the guards.

Create a Congressional Commemorative Observance

IN EVERY SESSION of Congress, dozens of commemorative resolutions are passed. Thus we have World Plumbing Day, National Day of Hope and Resolve, German American Day, and, of course, Mother's Day. When it comes to weeks, there is National Consumer Protection Week and National Nurses Week. There are even declarations that last a month: Slavery and Human Trafficking Prevention Month, Cancer Control Month, and Great Outdoors Month. In this activity, you will come up with a subject that is worthy of a day, week, or month of commemoration and create a collage to celebrate it.

Materials
★ Scissors
★ Photographs and illustrations cut from magazines, travel guides, brochures, fliers, catalogs, maps, postcards, greeting cards, stamps, and newspapers
★ Marker
★ Poster board, 11 × 17 inches
★ Glue stick
★ Decorative items such as pieces of fabric, lace, ribbon, buttons, sewing scraps, stickers, dried flowers, or other small natural items
★ Camera
★ Paper and pen

1. Choose a topic for your congressional commemoration. Decide whether it should be for a day, a week, or a month. How about National Bicycle Safety Week or National Walk Barefoot Day (to show how it feels to have no shoes to wear)?

2. Find and cut out pictures and drawings of items that illustrate your theme and that you find interesting. For example, if you were commemorating National Walk Barefoot Day, you might include pictures of drawings of people around the world who are barefoot because they cannot afford to buy shoes.

3. Use the marker to write the title of your Congressional Commemorative Observance on the poster board. Glue the pictures and drawings to the poster board and decorate with pieces of fabric, lace, shells, and so on.

4. Present your Congressional Commemorative Observance to your class.

5. Take a picture of your Congressional Commemorative Observance and send it to your congressional representative. Include a short letter explaining why you think the topic deserves a congressional commemorative resolution. Ask your representative to respond to your letter.

Women already had the right to vote in many states, granted by their state legislatures. By 1919, 15 states, mostly in the West, gave full voting rights to women. In another 12 states women could vote for president but not other federal offices. Twenty-one states denied women the right to vote at all.

The first attempt to pass a constitutional amendment granting universal suffrage, in 1868, went nowhere. Ten years later, when the issue was again brought up in the Senate, according to Senate records, "As suffragists pled their cause in the packed hearing room, committee members rudely read newspapers, or stared at the ceiling. Then they rejected the amendment."

In the last decades of the 19th century, the story remained the same. A solid block of southern senators, fearing a suffrage amendment

★ JEANNETTE RANKIN ★

Jeannette Rankin was the first woman elected to Congress. In 1916, she won an at-large seat (representing the entire state) in the House of Representatives from Montana, at a time when most women in America could not even vote. Later in life she was to say, "If I am remembered for no other act, I want to be remembered as the only woman who ever voted to give women the right to vote."

Rankin was also known as a pacifist, a person who would not vote for war. One of only 50 representatives to vote against America's entry into World War I, she famously declared, "As a woman, I can't go to war."

Defeated in her bid to be elected a senator from Montana in 1918, Rankin then devoted many years to social activism, particularly in New York City. Working with struggling immigrants on the Lower East Side of Manhattan, Rankin wrote to her mother about her wrenching experiences:

I took the dearest, sweetest little boy to an orphan society. He was about three- years-old and the mother had two younger. The father is missing. If I had been near home, I'm sure I would have wanted to keep him.

He was so full of joy and life. The mother didn't mind losing him. She just waved her hand and said, "bye-bye."

In 1940, Jeannette Rankin was again elected to the House of Representatives from Montana. Her pacifist beliefs undiminished, she was the only member of Congress to vote against the country's entry into World War II, following the December 7, 1941, Japanese attack on Pearl Harbor. So outraged were many fellow representatives, Rankin was chased out of the House chamber and forced to hide in a telephone booth, where she called congressional police to rescue her.

Rankin never again ran for Congress. Instead she devoted the rest of her long life to peace. In 1985, a statue of Jeannette Rankin, representing Montana, was placed in the US Capitol's Statuary Hall.

Portrait of the first woman to be elected to the House of Representatives, Jeannette Rankin.
Library of Congress LC-cph 3a113

would extend voting rights to black women, derailed any proposal. Others were concerned that granting women the right to vote would only encourage them on the Prohibition front.

By 1919, however, a lot had changed in America. The Progressive Era, with passage of three constitutional amendments (16th, 17th, and 18th), was reaching its summit. In 1918, the House of Representatives passed a suffrage amendment, on a 274 to 136 vote—only one more than needed for the two-thirds requirement.

In order to gain the necessary Senate votes, President Woodrow Wilson, on September 30, 1918, went to Capitol Hill and addressed the Senate in a 15-minute speech. "We have made partners of the women in this war [World War I]," he said. "Shall we admit them only to a partnership of suffering and sacrifice and toil, and not to a partnership of privilege and right?" The president's speech failed to win the additional two votes necessary for Senate approval.

But a new Congress in 1919 increased the amendment's supporters. The 19th Amendment passed both houses of Congress in May and gained the 36 states needed to meet the two-thirds requirement 14 months later. Women everywhere were finally allowed to vote in the national election of 1920.

Learn How to Register to Vote

WHILE YOU MAY not be old enough to vote, it is never too early to understand how registering to vote is done in your state. In this activity, you will determine the voter registration requirements for a given state. You may choose the state you live in, or, for comparison, any other state. Once you have the information, prepare a one- or two-page report that explains the requirements and the process.

Materials
★ Access to a computer with printer
★ Paper and pen or pencil

1. Go to the USA.gov (government made easy) website at www.usa.gov/Citizen/Topics/Voting/Register.shtml.

2. Under "Register to Vote," you will see a sentence that says, "You may be able to apply to register to vote in person at the following public facilities." Select "election offices."

3. Note, it says, "United States Election Assistance Commission" at the top. Where it says "Contact Your State," choose the state you want to gather data from. The information you obtain will go into your report.

4. Find where it indicates "qualifications" or "eligibility." List the qualifications to register.

5. See if there are any voter registration deadlines. If so, note them.

6. See if the state you have chosen allows one to register to vote on the day of an election. If so, you will need to provide proof of residence. List the choices for that proof.

7. List the places where one can pick up a voter registration application. In some states, it is possible to complete a voter registration form online. See if the state you have chosen allows this and note the answer.

8. With the data you have gathered, write a report describing the voter registration process. Be as creative as you like, just as long as you have answered five basic questions regarding voter registration in your state: (1) What are the qualifications to register? (2) What are the voter registration deadlines? (3) Can one register to vote on Election Day? (4) Where can one obtain a registration application? (5) Can one complete the voter registration process online?

9. Through classroom discussion and exchange, you may want to compare your state results with others. Are most states basically alike? Are there any significant differences?

Irish American immigrants sent a portion of their wages to relatives in Ireland. In some cases, these wages provided their only income.

COMING TO AMERICA
Congress and Immigration Policy

The US Congress has been dealing with immigration from the moment the legislative branch was created. In 1790, Congress adopted uniform rules so that free white persons could apply for citizenship. In 1875, the Supreme Court declared the regulation of immigration was a federal, that is, congressional, responsibility. In 1891, in response to a massive increase in immigration, the Immigration Service was established. Congress has been acting as an immigration gatekeeper from its beginnings to this day.

Looking back, our nation's first real surge in immigration came as the result of a tragedy that nearly wiped out an entire people. The Irish potato famines of the 1840s forced tens of thousands to flee on "famine ships" to America.

Upon arrival, the Irish, being Catholics, experienced stinging discrimination from an American Protestant population. They quickly found themselves on the bottom of the social and economic ladder, at least on the East Coast.

On the West Coast, it was Chinese workers, brought in to build the country's railroads, who felt the brunt of prejudice. The phrase "He doesn't stand a Chinaman's chance" basically said it all about where the Chinese were in the social pecking order.

In 1882, Congress passed the Chinese Exclusion Act, which placed a 10-year halt to Chinese labor immigration. The act became the first federal law to limit immigration of a specific ethnic group. The Chinese Exclusion Act was based on the assumption that Chinese laborers were upsetting "the good order of certain localities within the territory." The expulsion was extended for another 10 years in 1892 and made permanent by an act of Congress in 1902. (Only in 1943, with China an ally of the United States during World War II, did Congress finally repeal the Chinese Exclusion Act.)

Finding a Formula

By the end of World War I (in 1919) Americans were tired—weary of foreign wars and with

most things foreign. Above all, they wanted a retreat from world responsibilities. Americans hungered for a return to the usual. Campaigning for the presidency in 1920, Senator Warren G. Harding of Ohio declared: "America's present need is not heroics, but healing; not nostrums [cure-alls], but normalcy; not revolution, but restoration." The country's desire to be more isolated extended to restrictions on immigration. Most Americans wanted less of it.

Representative Albert Johnson, Republican of Washington, sponsored a new, far-reaching law that would severely limit immigration. Known as the Emergency Quota Act of 1921, it passed the Senate on a 78–1 vote and the House without a vote even being recorded. The act, according to one historian, would be "the most important turning-point in American immigration policy."

The Emergency Quota Act did two things that no other law on immigration had yet done. One, it set limits on the number of people who could emigrate from Europe and, two, used a quota (percentage) system in establishing those limits. From now on, the maximum number of immigrants admitted from a given country annually would be limited to 3 percent of the number of residents from that country living in the United States as of the US Census of 1910. In 1920, 805,228 immigrants entered the United States. In 1921–1922, with the act

Research Ellis Island Records

THERE ARE MANY entry points where those wishing to immigrate to the United States have arrived. Los Angeles and San Francisco are key destinations on the West Coast. Many arrivals from Asia enter through these ports, be it by ship or by airplane. On the East Coast, the main point of arrival for nearly a century was Ellis Island, in New York Harbor.

If you believe your ancestors might have come to the United States via Ellis Island, this activity will help you to find out. You will go to the Ellis Island website and determine if someone you know came through Ellis Island sometime between 1892 and 1924.

Materials
★ Access to a computer with a printer

1. Go to the Ellis Island website at www.ellisisland.org. Click on "Sign In" in the upper right corner. If you are new to the site, click on "Yes, I am new to this site." With a parent or guardian's permission, fill out the basic information asked for.

2. Go back to the site's home page and call up the "Passenger Search" pull-down menu in the upper left. Select "Search Tips." Read the material over, particularly the discussion on doing a "broad to narrow" search.

3. Return to the "Passenger Search" pull-down menu and select "Advanced Search." As best you can, fill in the information for the person you are looking for. The more fields you can complete, the better chance of finding a match. If you can't think of anyone to look for, pick a famous person. You may need to go on the web to find biographical information about the individual, such as when he or she was born, where the person was born, etc. EXAMPLE: Betty Hope, female, born in 1901, arrived in the United States in 1910, and came from the town of Leigh, England.

4. Click on "Start Search." Chances are you will come up with a "No exact matches for this passenger" statement. Scroll down to the list of last names and highlight the top one (broader search). Click on "Search on the checked name choice." NOTE: You may have to do this twice to bring up a list of names.

5. Find the individual you are looking for. EXAMPLE: number 157, Betty Hope. Call up the individual's "Passenger Record," "Ship Manifest," and "Ship Image," printing each one out as you go.

6. Using the documents you have printed, prepare a brief summary of the person whose immigration history you have uncovered.

in place, immigration dropped to 309,556 individuals. Hardest hit, as was intended, were those seeking entry from eastern and southern Europe.

The Emergency Quota Act of 1921 was soon followed with the Immigration Act of 1924, which went even further in cutting off entry. Now the quota was reduced to 2 percent and the census used to determine the actual numbers was pushed backed to 1890. Middle Easterners, East Asians, and Indians were barred completely. Opposition by Congress to the 1924 act was said to be minimal.

It would take more than 40 years before another immigration act appeared that, again, altered significantly the way the United States of America admits those seeking permanent residency. Known as the Immigration Act of 1965, it phased out the national origins quota method first put into effect in 1921 and substituted a new system. That new procedure is, with minor changes, still in effect today. From now on, more individuals would be admitted from third world (less developed) countries, such as India and Pakistan, with no national limitations.

The 1965 act (implemented on July 1, 1968) replaced the quota system with one that emphasized job skills and family reunification. The act was seen as an extension of civil rights views (prominent in the mid-1960s) to beyond American borders. The House passed the Immigration Act of 1965 by a vote of 326–69, and the Senate 76–18.

At the time of its passage, many members of Congress and the Johnson administration were quick to assure Americans that little change would occur in the number and mix of those who would now enter the country. Attorney

★ THE SENATE "GANG OF EIGHT" ★

In the summer of 2013, the US Senate's "Gang of Eight" had concluded their work. Made up of four Democrats and four Republicans (including big-name senators such as Charles E. Schumer, Democrat from New York, and John McCain, Republican of Arizona), the eight had worked out a bipartisan approach to broad immigration reform. The Senate's final bill passed with a 68–32 vote.

Among other things (the bill was 1,200 printed pages), the government would spend $46 billion (10 times the amount originally proposed) to beef up border security. An additional 20,000 border patrol agents would be hired—enough to place a guard (if all were employed at the same time) every 250 feet along the 2,000-mile border separating the United States from Mexico. The legislation as written provides $4.5 billion for drones and a double-layer fence along most of the border. The stated goal of the bill is to stop 90 percent of illegal entries. Immigrants who then agreed to pay a fine, work, and learn English would, in 10 years, be able to apply for permanent legal status. Finally, after a total of 13 years, they could become US citizens.

In exchange for this path to citizenship, the bill contends, illegal immigration would be reduced by legalizing it for some groups. For farm laborers there would be guest worker programs. And for employers needing them, highly skilled professionals would also be allowed entry.

The bill seemed to have something for everyone. But the House of Representatives was not buying it. The Republican leadership declared that they would come up with their own plan.

Take an American Citizenship Test

SUPPOSE, regardless of whether you were born in the United States or not, you were required to take a test to become a citizen. Such civics tests are given regularly by the US Citizenship and Immigration Services (USCIS) to those seeking American citizenship. The civics test is an oral test given by a USCIS officer who asks the applicant up to 10 of 100 civics questions. In this activity you will learn whether you could pass a US citizenship test!

Materials
★ Access to a computer

Answer the questions below and compare your answers with those given at the bottom of the page. If you get six or more correct answers, you pass the test.

Sample Test Questions

1. What is the supreme law of the land?
2. How many amendments does the Constitution have?
3. Who is in charge of the executive branch?
4. A US senator is elected for how many years?
5. A US representative is elected for how many years?
6. In what month do we vote for president?
7. Who vetoes bills?
8. Who wrote the Declaration of Independence?
9. Before he was president, Eisenhower was a general in what war?
10. What movement tried to end racial discrimination?

Below is a list of websites that provide free citizen naturalization tests with 100 questions and answers. Why not visit a site and see if you can answer all 100 questions? For additional websites with naturalization test questions, simply do a web search with the key words: US Citizen Naturalization Test.

Sample Civics Questions for US Citizenship or Naturalization
www.immihelp.com/citizenship/new-natural ization-test.html

US Naturalization Test Questions
www.funnelbrain.com/c-10249-does -constitution-do.html

Could you pass a US citizenship test?
www.csmonitor.com/USA/2011/0104 /Could-you-pass-a-US-citizenship-test /Who-signs-bills

A Sample 100 Question Citizenship Test
cltr.co.douglas.nv.us/Elections /100QuestionTest.htm

USCIS Study Materials for the Civics Test
www.uscis.gov/citizenship/learners/study-test /study-materials-civics-test

Answers to questions 1–10:
1. the Constitution
2. 27
3. the president
4. 6
5. 2
6. November
7. the president
8. Thomas Jefferson
9. World War II
10. civil rights (movement)

General Robert Kennedy predicted that immigration from Asia "would virtually disappear."

Kennedy's prediction was wrong. The new act shifted the balance from European to non-European countries. From 1901 to 1920, 4 percent of those entering the United States as immigrants came from Asian countries. Thirty years later, the percentage had grown to 39 percent.

Of course, all the above data refers to legal immigration. For many Americans, who comes from where, legally, is of little concern. Not so with those arriving and staying here illegally.

Immigrants enter the country at Ellis Island in the early 1900s by walking across a bridge.
Library of Congress LC-cph 3b46739

A Pathway to Citizenship

IN 2011, an estimated 11.5 million people were living in the United States illegally. With a total population of 312 million, that number represented 3.7 percent. By illegal, it is meant individuals who either entered the country without papers (they snuck across the border), or who had overstayed their visas (they came in legally on condition they remain for a given period of time, but have illegally extended their stay). Of those here illegally, 62 percent have come from Mexico. The vast majority entered by crossing, at various points, the 2,000-mile border between Mexico and the United States.

Congress has sought to deal with illegal immigration in a number of ways. Almost all efforts have taken a piecemeal approach: a stronger border fence here, a temporary guest worker program (allowing foreign workers to work and reside in a host country temporarily) there. People on both sides of the issue are dissatisfied with these measures. What is needed, say pro- and anti-immigration groups alike, is broader, more sweeping immigration reform. Getting members of Congress to agree on what that means has been a laborious task.

To begin with, there is the issue of terminology. Should those not here legally be called "illegal aliens" or "undocumented immigrants"? Then there is the word "amnesty" (a pardon to a large group of individuals). For some, granting amnesty to those here illegally is a good thing for them and for America. Others disagree. To them, giving someone amnesty rewards illegal behavior and is unfair to those who obey the law and go through processes to enter the country legally.

Should we round up and deport illegal immigrants? For some in Congress it would be as easy as one, two, three! One, go to where you know they are; two, arrest them; three, deport them. Yet, as Senator John McCain, Republican of Arizona, says, he has "yet to hear a single proponent of this point of view offer one realistic proposal for locating, apprehending, and returning to their countries of origin over 11 million people."

These are just some of the issues Congress grapples with in searching for a solution to illegal immigration. These, and many more matters, must be addressed if any comprehensive solution is to be achieved.

For most members of Congress, the question centers on the issue of a "pathway to citizenship." Democrats overwhelmingly favor such a course, even if it could take an individual 13 years to achieve it. Most Republicans say no—that is still amnesty, and amnesty rewards illegal behavior.

To a large extent, a member's views on the matter reflect the ethnic makeup of his or her **constituency**. If a member of Congress represents a district with a sizable percentage of Latinos, obviously that is a factor. Republican Jeff Denham serves a Central Valley farming district in California. The district's population is 40 percent Latino. Most come, and are needed, to work picking the crops. Denham, who is married to the daughter of a legal Mexican immigrant, has said, "I witnessed the trials and the joys of immigration through my own family." The congressman tends to favor a pathway to citizenship.

Denham's fellow Republican representative from California, Dana Rohrabacher, whose Orange County district is only 20 percent Latino, declared, "We do not need more people from foreign countries coming in and taking the jobs of Americans. . . . I say let the prisoners pick the fruits."

Where there seems to be some common ground, where both Democrats and Republicans might come together, is over the issue of "dreamers." Dreamers are the estimated 1.7 million young individuals classified as illegal because they were brought to the United States by parents who are not here legally. They seek a special status that will allow them to pursue their educational and career dreams. They put their hopes in a DREAM Act.

DREAMers and the DREAM Act

Antonio Cisnero lives in Pomona, California. He was born in Acapulco, Mexico. Antonio has no legal status—he is an undocumented immigrant. When asked about his dreams, he replied, "I am on my way to obtaining an electrical engineering degree from California State University, Los Angeles." Cisnero then went on to say, "As of now I have a full-time job and go to school. I pay for all my tuition and books because I do not qualify for loans. . . . I will keep on going to school until I have obtained my bachelor's degree."

Meron Mengistu is also an American with no legal status. She lives in Washington, DC, and was born in Ethiopia. "Currently I am in graduate school," she said. "I hope to finish my education before the age of 27 and be able to work in the USA."

Regemralph Corpuz is from the Philippines but is currently living in Encino, California. When finished with college he wants to work in the government or media. "I hope to take advantage of the new deferred action passed and continue being a great student. I will also continue being a strong activist for the undocumented community and keep fighting for our rights and keep pushing for the DREAM Act."

These youngsters, and the others like them, are known as DREAMers. They were born in a foreign country but were brought here, in the vast majority of cases, with their parents. Since their parents are here illegally, the children are noncitizens; they are undocumented.

Antonio, Meron, and Regemralph are able to attend college because they benefit from a program known as Deferred Action for Childhood Arrivals (DACA), announced by the Obama administration in the summer of 2012. Under DACA, for example, if you were brought here as a child, you can get protection from deportation. You can also petition for a work permit. But to qualify, you must be currently in school or the military and have no criminal record.

When President Obama signed off on DACA, he did so by bypassing Congress. DACA is considered a temporary program, one unlikely to remain in effect when the president leaves office. What DREAMers want is an act of Congress that would make the above provisions (plus many more) permanent. Known as the DREAM Act (Development, Relief, and Education for Alien Minors), a version of it passed the House of Representatives on December 8, 2012, by a vote of 216–198. It failed in the Senate, however.

A DREAM act of some type represents the best chance for Democrats and Republicans to come together on immigration reform. Still, with congresspeople and the public holding strong feelings on both sides of the issue, it will not be easy.

★ ★ ★ ★ ★ ★ ★ ★ ★ ★ ★

★ MARCO RUBIO ★

Senator Marco Rubio, Republican of Florida, is a Cuban American who was born in Miami on May 28, 1971. He is considered by many to be the "crown prince of the **Tea Party** movement." As such, Senator Rubio is politically quite conservative. Even though the senator took office on January 3, 2011, by mid-2013 he was being seriously talked about as a presidential contender in 2016. If Marco Rubio were to obtain that highest of offices, he would be the first Hispanic to do so.

What prompted the discussion of a presidential candidacy was Senator Rubio's role in immigration reform. As one of eight senators (four Republicans and four Democrats) making up the "Senate Gang of Eight," in the early part of 2013, the senator played a key role in putting together a bipartisan Senate proposal for comprehensive immigration reform. The plan suggested a path to citizenship for illegal immigrants that included the payment of fines and back taxes, background checks, and a lengthy probationary period, among other features.

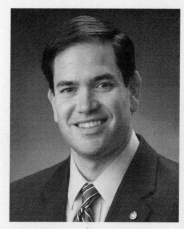

Marco Rubio, senator from Florida, believes in comprehensive immigration reform. Wikimedia Commons

In a speech delivered on the Senate floor on June 26, 2013, Senator Rubio got personal about immigration. Talking about immigrants in general, but also specifically about his father (who emigrated from Cuba in 1956), the Senator said:

They have come because in the land of their birth, their dreams were bigger than their opportunities. Here they brought their language and their customs, their religions and their music, and somehow they made them ours as well.... Go to our factories and our fields, go to the kitchens and construction sites, go to the cafeterias in this very capitol and there you will find that the miracle of America is still alive. For here in America those who once had no hope will give their kids the chance at a life they always wanted for themselves. Here in America generations of unfulfilled dreams will finally come to pass.

On Pennsylvania Avenue His con-
tuents give him a sudden shock.

The waiter, to
, looks like a
man.

MARK

A "nervous congressman" suspects everyone he meets to be a spy investigating him.

r. He is con-
the lady he is
wn is a female

His private office — but no privacy.

The little children make a noise like a secret service agent.

A friend returns a borrowed ten, but he rejects it. He fears marked money.

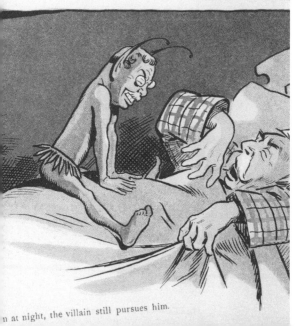

n at night, the villain still pursues him.

★ 6 ★

KEEPING A WATCHFUL EYE
Congress Investigates

In response to Native American attacks on white settlers in the summer of 1791, President George Washington ordered General Arthur St. Clair into the Ohio Valley, in what was then known as the Northwest Territory. The general was instructed to seek out and fight Chief Little Turtle of the Miamis. The resulting conflict, known fittingly as the Battle of a Thousand Slain, ended in the greatest US Army defeat by Native Americans and the worst calamity US forces ever suffered in *any* battle—ever.

Both opposing camps were evenly matched with approximately 1,000 men. St. Clair's forces, however, were weighed down with an additional 200 to 250 women and children, nearly all of whom would be killed. Inadequately supplied and dangerously underestimating enemy strength, St. Clair led his men into the fight on November 4, 1791; only 48 escaped unharmed. In the fight that lasted just three hours, approximately one-quarter of the entire US Army was wiped out.

When General St. Clair returned to the US capital, President Washington demanded his resignation. Soon after, the House of Representatives began its own investigation into the disaster. This was the first such probe Congress had ever undertaken. A congressional committee would request, and eventually receive, documents from the executive branch dealing with the affair. In the end, Congress cleared St. Clair of any blame in the disaster. In gaining the documents it needed, however, Congress established its right to investigate the executive branch.

Congress has, over the last 200-plus years, vigorously investigated just about anything it wants. Known as congressional oversight, this wide range of activities includes scandals, crime, national security, health, education, compliance and regulatory issues, and corporate America. While the Constitution does not explicitly (openly) grant Congress the authority to conduct inquiries or investigations of the executive, the right to do so is implied (given indirectly). After all, Congress cannot legislate without knowing what the executive is doing. It must understand how programs are being administered, by whom, and at what cost, and whether the law is being obeyed.

Today, in addition to its oversight of the executive, Congress uses investigations to gather information in drafting legislation. It does so to inform and educate the public. Furthermore, Congress scrutinizes in order to police itself. And its investigations often act as safety valves, by allowing potentially disruptive issues to be decided in a hearing room rather than out in the streets.

In carrying out its investigative functions, Congress will often subpoena an individual, that is, compel a witness to appear before it. Failure to respond positively to a subpoena can leave a person in contempt of Congress, which may result in severe legal penalties.

While high-profile investigations get all the media attention, it is worth noting that such undertakings represent a small portion of Congress's total oversight and investigation efforts.

"Have you no decency?"

DETERMINED CONGRESSIONAL investigations of communist activities began in the 1930s. The Soviet Union's "alternative" socialist approach to government and economics grew in appeal as the American capitalist system came under strain during the Great Depression. In response, Congress established a special investigating committee, known as the Dies Committee, after its first chairman, Representative Martin Dies, Democrat of Texas. The committee's stated purpose was "To investigate the extent, character, and objectives of un-American propaganda activities in the United States." In 1945, the Dies Committee became a standing (permanent) committee. It was renamed the House Un-American Activities Committee (HUAC).

Wisconsin Senator Joseph McCarthy was not, as many people believe, a member of the House Un-American Activities Committee. The HUAC was a House of Representatives creation. McCarthy was not a member of the lower chamber. He was a US senator.

However, it can be argued that no one in the House was ever as anticommunist as Joseph McCarthy. Born in Grand Chute, Wisconsin, in 1908, McCarthy attended a one-room school through the eighth grade, left to work on a farm, then returned to school, graduating from Little Wolf High School, in the town of Manawa, at the age of 21. Determined, dedicated, and hardworking, McCarthy went on to earn a law degree, be elected a circuit judge, and serve in the US Marine Corps. In 1946 he won election to the US Senate as a conservative Republican, edging out the state's legendary progressive senator, Robert La Follette, in the Republican primary.

McCarthy's rise to national fame began on February 9, 1950, when the then 42-year-old senator delivered a Lincoln Day address in

Find Congressional Images at the Library of Congress

THE LIBRARY OF CONGRESS (LOC) contains over 100 million items, a huge number of which are photos, prints, and drawings. These could be helpful for you to use sometime in a school report or presentation. In this activity, you will learn how to search the LOC database for images dealing with congressional history. A drawing illustrating the impeachment of President Andrew Johnson is used here as an example to guide you through the process. Once you get the hang of it, you will see how easy it is to use this incredible resource (the LOC) to obtain images.

Materials
★ Access to a computer with a printer

1. Go to the Library of Congress (LOC) website at www.loc.gov. Under "Search," select "Photos, Prints, Drawings."

2. Under "Search Loc.gov" write "impeachment of President Andrew Johnson" and select "Go."

3. Scroll to "The Smelling Committee" print.

4. Select "The Smelling Committee" print. Note that under the "About This Item" tab, the "Rights Advisory" says: "No known restrictions on publication." This usually means that the public can use the image.

5. Explore the various tabs. Under "About This Item" you can read a summary or description of what is in the image. "Obtaining Copies" describes various methods of obtaining the image. If you want "Access to Original," you will need to fill out a call slip and, of course, go to the Library of Congress, in Washington, DC.

6. Beneath the image to the left, select "View Larger." A much larger image will appear that you can download or print, free of charge.

7. Select a subject in this book that interests you. By repeating the steps above, see what images are available concerning that subject. Select other subjects and repeat the process.

Wheeling, West Virginia. In his speech, McCarthy declared: "I have in my hand a list of 205 ... a list of names that were made known to the Secretary of State as being members of the Communist Party and who nevertheless are still working and shaping policy in the State Department." Later McCarthy would modify that number, reducing it to 57.

Regardless of how many suspected individuals there supposedly were, Senator McCarthy was unable to produce the name of a single communist in any government office. He never made his list public. Nonetheless, the brash and determined senator was on his way. With the national media spotlight squarely on him, McCarthy would hunt out subversives; "reds," in the government wherever he suspected they existed—and that would be just about everywhere.

Having been reelected senator in 1952, McCarthy charged ahead with his "red-baiting" as chair of the Permanent Subcommittee on Investigations (both the Senate and the House have subcommittees to distribute the work of main committees to various members; subcommittees handle specific areas of main committee work). In 1953, the subcommittee, under McCarthy's leadership, held a series of dramatic hearings where the senator personally bullied witnesses and intimidated senators who opposed him. In doing so, McCarthy disrupted the Senate's normal rules, customs, and decorum. The senator didn't care. He claimed his no-holds-barred approach was necessary to combat communist subversion.

In 1954, Senator McCarthy, at the height of his influence, chose to take on the US Army. During his inquiry, McCarthy verbally assaulted Brigadier General Ralph W. Zwicker, a highly decorated war hero. The senator from Wisconsin accused the general of not having even "the brains of a five-year-old" and of

★ COMIC BOOK INQUISITION ★

While Senator Joseph McCarthy was busy probing for communists in the federal government, another congressional investigation committee was seeking to establish a link between juvenile delinquency and comic books. At the time, in 1954, it was estimated that more than 20 comic book publishers were putting out close to 650 titles a month. Eighty to 100 million comic books were sold every week. A third of all comic books were horror comics, with titles such as *Chamber of Chills, The Tormented, Tomb of Terror,* and *Tales from the Crypt.* The Senate Subcommittee on Juvenile Delinquency, conducting three days of hearings, wanted to know if there was a link between comics and juvenile crime.

Meeting in New York City, on April 21, 1954, one witness, publisher William Gaines, asserted that he only published comic books within the bounds of good taste. Senator Estes Kefauver, of Tennessee, responded by stating: "Here is your May issue. This seems to be a man with a bloody ax holding a woman's head up which has been severed from her body. Do you think that's in good taste?" Gaines responded: "Yes sir, I do—for the cover of a horror comic."

In response to the Senate Subcommittee on Juvenile Delinquency inquiry, with its probe of comic books, the comic book industry adopted the Comics Code Authority. This ratings code, with some alteration, is still in effect today.

being "not fit to wear that uniform." The senator strongly suggested that Zwicker should be relieved of duty for having shielded "traitors and communists." When transcripts of the private hearings were leaked to the media, American opinion turned sharply against McCarthy.

In response to McCarthy's assault against Zwicker, the army accused the senator of seeking special treatment for one of his staff members (David Schine), who had recently been drafted into the army. McCarthy agreed to step down temporarily as chair of the Permanent Subcommittee on Investigations to allow the committee to probe these charges.

In what became known as the Army-McCarthy hearings, 35 days of live TV coverage made it clear to 20 million viewers what McCarthy, now a witness himself, was like. In one famous exchange, Joseph N. Welch, chief lawyer for the army, declared: "Until this moment, Senator, I think I never really gauged your cruelty or your recklessness. . . . Have you no sense of decency, sir, at long last? Have you left no sense of decency?" When the hushed audience in the room burst into prolonged applause, a visibly shaken McCarthy turned to an aide and asked, "What happened?"

In December 1954, the full US Senate, in a vote of 67 to 22, censured Senator Joseph McCarthy for his conduct. Devastated, McCarthy never regained his influence. The senator from

Nominate Two People for National Statuary Hall

NATIONAL STATUARY HALL is located in the Capitol Building, next to the Rotunda. The Hall contains statues that honor men and women who are "illustrious for their historic renown." Teachers, legislators, peacemakers, warriors, inventors, and explorers have been featured in National Statuary Hall. All states now have two statues as part of their National Statuary Hall display. In this activity, you will select two people who you think deserve to represent your state in National Statuary Hall.

Materials
★ Access to a computer with a printer

1. In Statuary Hall, there are two statues for each state. To find out who is featured from your state, go to the US House of Representatives: History, Art & Archives: National Statuary Hall Collection at http://history.house.gov/Exhibitions-and-Publications/Statuary-Hall/Hall/Statues/.

2. Under the "Viewing" pull-down menu, select and click on your state. Choose two new individu-als who you think should be featured. There are a number of sources you can use to find a brief history of individuals of note in your state. In addition to the Internet, try your school library.

3. Once you have selected an individual, do a search on his or her name, followed by the words: "image of." For example, if you want a photograph of William Mulholland, a well-known California engineer who built a huge aqueduct in the state, type in "William Mulholland, image of."

4. Create a short report about your candidate. Title your report "A Candidate for National Statuary Hall," followed by the name of your state. Copy and paste an image of your selected individual into your report.

5. Write two or three paragraphs on who the individual is and why he or she should be given the honor of representing your state in National Statuary Hall. Repeat these steps for your second candidate.

Wisconsin died on May 2, 1957, from cirrhosis of the liver, a disease usually associated with heavy alcohol consumption.

"A third-rate burglary"?

ANOTHER HISTORIC US Congressional investigation, one with equal if not more significance, took place in the mid-1970s. On May 17, 1973, the bipartisan Senate Select Committee on Presidential Campaign Activities, commonly known as the Watergate Committee, opened the first of its public hearings. Senator Sam Ervin of North Carolina chaired the committee. The hearings were held in the Senate Caucus Room, the same place that had held the Army-McCarthy hearings two decades earlier. As with those early 1950s hearings, the Watergate Committee would be widely covered on television.

On June 17 of the previous year, five men had broken into the Democratic National Committee headquarters at the Watergate hotel and office complex in Washington, DC. In addition to carrying $3,500 in cash, the burglars were loaded down with high-end surveillance and electronics equipment. The five were there to bug the office headquarters.

When, on January 10, 1973, the trial of the Watergate burglars began, most Americans assumed what had occurred on June 17 was essentially a "third-rate burglary." However, after weeks of trial testimony, Chief Federal District Judge John Sirica came to the conclusion that not all the facts in the case had been revealed. The judge urged those awaiting sentencing to cooperate with the soon-to-be-established Senate select committee.

The Senate Watergate Committee is credited with reviving public confidence in congressional investigations. That faith, as has been shown, had suffered during the McCarthy inquiries of the early 1950s. The committee's success was due to "extensive media coverage, sustained public interest, the meticulous work of investigators, the cooperation of key witnesses, and the continuing support of the full Senate," it was now being reported in the media.

Throughout the hearings, President Richard Nixon refused to cooperate. He insisted that the separation of powers spelled out in the Constitution meant his aides should not be required to testify or that any White House papers should be made available to the committee. Eventually, Nixon agreed to let aides participate, but still the president refused to hand over documents. When it was revealed that voice-activated tapes existed, documenting practically everything that went on in the White House, Sam Ervin requested access to the tapes. Previously, a White House assistant testified that the president had approved plans to cover up executive branch connections to the break-in—a federal crime.

When the Watergate Committee demanded the tapes, Nixon declined to turn them over, again citing executive privilege. Senator Ervin responded by pointing out that the Constitution gave Congress the power to investigate and required that the president cooperate.

The Supreme Court agreed. On July 24, the court ruled unanimously that the president must surrender the tapes. President Nixon complied, and the tapes revealed that he had approved a plan to cover up the White House connection to the Watergate burglary. As a result, the House Judiciary Committee adopted three articles of impeachment against the president. Before a vote was taken, Nixon resigned the presidency on August 9, 1974.

A Clear Edge on the Field

FROM WATERGATE to baseball may seem like a long throw, but by the first decade of the 21st century, Congress was willing to investigate almost anything. Our national pastime was not to be overlooked.

Known by many baseball fans as the "40–40 man," one-time American League MVP (Most Valuable Player) Jose Canseco was, many claimed, unsurpassed in both power and speed. Such a combination allowed Canseco to become the first man in baseball history to blast out more than 40 home runs and steal more

than 40 bases in the same season. Where did all that strength and quickness come from? With publication, in 2006, of his tell-all book, *Juiced: Wild Times, Rampant 'Roids, Smash Hits, and How Baseball Got Big*, the world would find out—though most with any interest in Major League Baseball already knew the answer. Performance-enhancing drugs (PEDs), particularly steroids, had given not only Canseco but also a host of other baseball stars a clear edge on the field of play.

Senator Sam Ervin (third from left), of North Carolina, chairs the Senate Select Committee, known as the Watergate Committee. Wally McNamee/CORBIS WL8829

Partly in response to the revelations in *Juiced*, Congress opened hearings into the use of PEDs in professional baseball. Representative Henry Waxman (Democrat from California), a member of the powerful US House Committee on Oversight and Government Reform, took the lead in scolding professional baseball's leadership for not adequately policing itself with regard to PED use by its players. With respect to Canseco's revelations, according to congressional testimony, "Sandy Alderson, a senior Major League official, said, 'I'd be surprised if there were any serious follow-up.'" Bud Selig, commissioner of Major League Baseball at the time, was quoted as saying, "As a sport, we have done everything that we could."

The Oversight and Government Reform Committee is one of the most influential and powerful committees in the House of Representatives. The committee is Congress's chief investigative and oversight entity. It is granted broad jurisdiction. The chairman of the committee is the only committee chair in the entire House who can, if he or she wishes, issue subpoenas without a committee vote.

There are those who have questioned the right of the Oversight and Government Reform Committee, or any other congressional committee for that matter, to investigate the doings of professional baseball. According to one poll, taken in March 2005, only 22 percent of respondents felt that Congress had any business injecting itself into the affairs of Major League Baseball.

Yet the Reform Committee clearly has the authority to conduct hearings on any subject falling under the jurisdiction of Congress. In the 1950s (the heyday of congressional investigations), Congress held hearings not only into communists but also juvenile delinquency, the Mafia, music industry payola (undercover payouts), quiz shows, and comic books.

Furthermore, it is argued that Congress can and should investigate the use of performance-enhancing drugs by professional athletes, be

An 1894 Temple Cup playoff game between the Baltimore Orioles and the New York Giants at the Polo Grounds in New York.

Library of Congress LC-DIG-ppmsca-18838

they baseball players or any other type of players. After all, the issue touches on such public policy concerns as health, drug abuse, and drug trafficking.

As we have seen, aside from its legislative activities, Congress devotes a great deal of attention to investigations. Though the Constitution provides no express power for Congress to investigate, the institution has always acted on the assumption that it has such authority. Congressional investigations are a critical part of our system of checks and balances.

★ HARRY S. TRUMAN ★

Before Harry Truman became the 33rd president of the United States, he was the country's 34th vice president, and before that, a US senator from Missouri. Elected to the Senate in 1934, Truman served in the upper chamber until January 17, 1945. Three days later, he became President Franklin D. Roosevelt's vice president. When Roosevelt died in office, on April 12, 1945, Truman became president.

In his first bid for a Senate seat, Truman, a Democrat, defeated the **incumbent** (sitting) Republican, Roscoe C. Patterson, by nearly 20 percentage points. In his first term as a US senator, Truman, true to his party's tradition, spoke out against Wall Street and moneyed special interests as having too much influence in national affairs.

Before Harry S. Truman became president, he was a US senator from Missouri.
Library of Congress Reproduction Number: LC-DIG-hec-23496

As a senator, Truman gained a reputation going after waste and profiteering (making an unreasonable profit) during World War II. As the nation prepared for war, Truman, as subcommittee chairman in the Committee on Military Affairs, began to investigate abuses. In a separate committee set up by Truman, which soon became known as the Truman Committee, the senator from Missouri became a national figure.

The Truman Committee, charged with investigating the National Defense Program, was reported to have saved as much as $15 billion. The committee's activities put Truman on the cover of *Time* magazine. It was said that no senator ever gained greater political benefits from chairing a special investigating committee than did Missouri's Harry Truman.

★ ★

African Americans carry signs for equal rights, integrated schools, decent housing, and an end to bias at a march on Washington, DC, on August 28, 1963. Library of Congress LC-DIG-ppmsca-3128

 7 ★

TIRED OF GIVING IN
Congress and Civil Rights

The freedom from unequal treatment on the basis of skin color, gender, religion, disability, or other protected characteristics is called civil rights. Civil rights are the rights of individuals to receive equal treatment, not to be discriminated against in a number of settings, such as education, employment, and housing, to name the most obvious. Historically, the Civil Rights Movement referred to efforts in achieving equality for African Americans in every aspect of society.

Rosa Parks Takes a Seat

IT IS not difficult to know where and when the post–World War II American civil rights movement to ban discrimination against African Americans began. It occurred on a cold December 1, in 1955, when a 42-year-old African American woman in Montgomery, Alabama, refused to give up her bus seat to a white man. For failing to do so, Rosa Parks was arrested and charged with violation of Chapter 6, Section 11, of the Montgomery City Code. The city regulation prohibited integration on its public transportation system. Buses were segregated by law. Rosa Parks refused to go along with such segregation.

What resulted from what Rosa Parks did that day became known as the Montgomery Bus Boycott. For months, black citizens in Montgomery, often to great sacrifice and inconvenience, refused to ride the city's buses. Suffering considerable financial hardship in turn, Montgomery's transit authorities finally gave in.

On November 13, 1956, the Supreme Court ruled that bus segregation was unconstitutional. Soon thereafter, on December 20, 1956, the 381-day Montgomery Bus Boycott ended, and along with it, segregation in the city's public transportation. A new American civil rights movement had begun.

Master Obstructionist

Rosa Parks's stand against segregation was just the beginning of the fight for civil rights in the 1950s. There were many persons, particularly in the South, opposed to African Americans gaining equal rights. Such individuals were segregationists—they sought to keep blacks and whites apart, particularly in public accommodations. Not surprisingly, many had their views represented in Congress. One congressman in particular, a conservative Democrat named Howard W. Smith, of Virginia, was their unrivaled champion.

In 1955, Congressman Smith became chairman of the powerful House of Representatives Committee on Rules. Thanks to Howard Smith, when a bill came up that he did not like, particularly one on civil rights, he refused to assign it a rule, thus killing it. The Rules Committee became known as "Judge Smith's graveyard."

In 1957, the first major 20th-century civil rights bill came before Congress. Smith took a vacation, to visit relatives in North Carolina. When the congressman returned, he worked out a deal with the Speaker of the House, Sam Rayburn. Smith would send forth a weakened civil rights bill if Rayburn would agree to cut several pending bills providing federal aid to various projects.

The result was the Civil Rights Act of 1957. Though the bill would prove weak and, in many ways, ineffective, it did create the Civil Rights Division in the Department of Justice and set up a Commission on Civil Rights. Being the first civil rights bill since 1875, the Civil Rights Act of 1957 was a start. But more needed to be done.

In its weakened state, the Civil Rights Act of 1957 was relatively easy to get through Congress. No one ever said that about its successor, the historic Civil Rights Act of 1964. It would take the impressive political skills of key politicians, the assassination of a president, and, perhaps, a serious miscalculation by a key player, Howard Smith, to bring the act about.

On June 19, 1963, President John F. Kennedy sent a civil rights bill to Congress. It passed the House Judiciary Committee on November 20. Two days later, President Kennedy was assassinated in Dallas, Texas. Lyndon Johnson, who had become Kennedy's vice president in 1961, assumed the presidency. With the nation in shock and full mourning, Johnson went before Congress and declared that there could be no better memorial to Kennedy than passage of his civil rights bill.

★ JIM CROW LAWS ★

Segregation in the South was built on what were known as Jim Crow laws. The laws were named after "Jump Jim Crow," an early-19th-century song-and-dance caricature of African Americans. Enforced between 1876 and 1965 throughout the South and border states, the laws called for "separate but equal" status for black Americans. In reality, the accommodations afforded blacks were always inferior to those provided to whites. Jim Crow legalized segregation.

Below are some examples of Jim Crow laws as they applied to marriage, public facilities, education, entertainment, and free speech:

Marriage
All marriages between a White person and a Negro, or between a White person and a person of Negro descent to the fourth generation inclusive, are hereby forever prohibited. (Florida)

Public Facilities
It shall be unlawful for a Negro and White person to play together or in company with each other at any game of pool or billiards. (Alabama)

No colored barber shall serve as a barber to White women or girls. (Georgia)

Education
The schools for White children and the schools for Negro children shall be conducted separately. (Florida)

Entertainment
All circuses, shows, and tent exhibitions, to which the attendance of . . . more than one race is invited or expected to attend shall provide for the convenience of its patrons not less than two ticket offices with individual ticket sellers, and not less than two entrances to the said performance, with individual ticket takers and receivers, and in the case of outside or tent performances, the said ticket offices shall not be less than twenty-five feet apart. (Louisiana)

Free Speech
Any person . . . who shall be guilty of printing, publishing or circulating printed, typewritten or written material urging or presenting for public acceptance or general information, arguments or suggestions in favor of social equality or of intermarriage between Whites and Negroes, shall be guilty of a misdemeanor and subject to fine or not exceeding five hundred dollars or imprisonment not exceeding six months or both. (Mississippi)

Take a Virtual Tour of Capitol Hill

THE ARCHITECT OF THE CAPITOL (AOC) is a federal agency responsible for the maintenance, operation, development, and preservation of the US Capitol Complex. The AOC has created an amazing virtual (computer-generated) tour of Capitol Hill. Going on the virtual tour is both entertaining and informative. If you ever plan to actually go to Capitol Hill, taking the virtual tour first is a good idea.

Materials

★ Access to a computer with a printer

1. Go to the Architect of the Capitol website at: www.house.gov/content/learn/partners/aoc .php. Select "Architect's Virtual Capitol." Once the data file loads, you will see three icons at the bottom of the page: "Discover," "Explore," and "Learn." Click on "Discover."

2. The site opens to: "Welcome to the AOC," a two-minute, 25-second multimedia presentation.

3. Sixteen icons appear at the top, including "Walking Tour of Capitol Campus" and "Constructing the Capitol Visitor Center."

4. Click on "Walking Tour of Capitol Campus." A three-minute, 30-second multimedia presentation begins. Take the tour.

5. EXPLORE!

---

illegal for employers to discriminate against women in the workplace.

There are those who claim that the aging representative from Virginia had a sneaky motive in mind when offering up the amendment. By adding "sex" to the Civil Rights Act of 1964, Smith, they insist, was actually trying to defeat the whole bill by including a measure he was confident his colleagues would oppose. If this was in fact Smith's motivation for introducing his amendment, then for once the representative miscalculated. In the end, the 1964 Civil Rights Act passed in the House by a 289–126 vote and in the Senate by 73–27 (with Smith's amendment). President Johnson immediately signed the bill into law.

While the Civil Rights Act of 1964 would produce profound changes in the way Americans lived and worked (especially in the South), more remained to be done. Still to be addressed was the key issue of voting rights for minorities.

At least one member of the lower house remained unmoved by President Johnson's plea: Howard Smith. To this day, historians are divided as to just what the then 81-year-old Smith was up to when he was quick to sponsor a curious addition to the civil rights bill. His simple amendment added the three-letter word "sex" to the bill's language, which would make it

The Power of the Ballot

A DECADE after Rosa Parks stood up, or, more accurately, sat down, in the fight for civil rights and integration, another notable protest—this one violent—occurred in the state of Alabama. Known as Bloody Sunday, on March 7, 1965, 600 marchers set out from Selma to Montgomery, on US Route 80. They got only as far as the

Edmund Pettus Bridge, six blocks from their starting point. On the bridge, state troopers and local police attacked the civil rights protestors, beating them with nightsticks, jabbing them with electric cattle prods, and spraying tear gas in their faces. The marchers were driven back into Selma, many bleeding in their retreat.

Two days later, Martin Luther King Jr. led a symbolic march to the bridge. And on March 21, 3,200 marchers, again led by King, set out from Selma for Montgomery. They walked 12 miles a day and slept in fields. By the time the marchers reached Montgomery, they were 25,000 strong. Five months later, President Lyndon Johnson signed the Voting Rights Act of 1965 into law.

Section 1 of the 15th Amendment to the US Constitution, passed in 1870 (five years after the Civil War ended), states:

The right of citizens of the United States to vote shall not be denied or abridged by the United States or by any State on account of race, color, or previous condition of servitude [slavery].

The 15th Amendment aside, it soon became apparent that many of the former Confederate states had no intention of spreading the right to

A crowd of 250,000 African Americans and whites surrounded the Reflecting Pool and continued to the Washington Monument on August 28, 1963.

Library of Congress LC-DIG-ppmsca-313

vote to African Americans. Through literacy tests, poll taxes, and other means, well into the 20th century, blacks were denied the ballot.

The Voting Rights Act of 1965, passed by Congress and signed into law by President Johnson, followed closely on the heels of the Civil Rights Act of 1964. The Voting Rights Act identified areas of the country where Congress believed the potential for discrimination in voting existed. Nine states were targeted—Alabama, Alaska, Arizona, Georgia, Louisiana, Mississippi, South Carolina, Texas, and Virginia. A number of counties throughout the nation (in other states) were also identified, such as Brooklyn, Manhattan, and the Bronx in New York State. These places were required by the act, in what was known as preclearance, to "receive clearance from the Justice Department or a federal court in Washington before they made minor changes to voting procedures, like moving a polling place, or major ones, like redrawing electoral districts."

On June 25, 2013, the US Supreme Court, in a 5–4 ruling, struck down the preclearance requirement of the Voting Rights Act. "Our country has changed," Chief Justice John G. Roberts Jr. wrote for the majority, as reported in the *New York Times*. "While any racial discrimination in voting is too much, Congress must ensure that the legislation it passes to remedy that problem speaks to current conditions."

Justice Roberts was saying that Congress was working with 40-year-old data. Today, Roberts pointed out, in many of the states first identified, African American voting rates are higher than those for white voters. Those justices voting in the majority were saying that Congress, in not having the political courage to update the states and districts where voting discrimination still exists, was not doing its job.

Civil rights leaders, including Martin Luther King Jr., in the front row, left of center, surrounded by crowds marching for civil rights, voting rights, jobs, decent housing, and more on August 28, 1963.

Library of Congress LC-DIG-ppmsca-4297

Make a Capitol Dome

THE DOME we now see on the Capitol Building is not the original dome. The current dome was completed shortly after the Civil War ended in 1865. Cast iron was used in its construction because it was less expensive and weighed much less than stone. The dome is painted white to look like white marble. In this activity, you will investigate the wonder of the triangle as a structural element in building a dome. Of course, many other structures, such as bridges and sports arenas, make use of the triangle as well. Triangle construction, as you will discover, adds tremendous strength to the building being erected. That's something the engineers designing the Capitol Building Dome were well aware of.

Materials
★ 32 toothpicks
★ 18 gumdrops

1. First construct a square and a triangle using gumdrops and toothpicks. You will need four gumdrops and four toothpicks to make the square. You will need three gumdrops and three toothpicks to make the triangle.

2. You have made the square and the triangle to test how much stronger a triangle is than a square. Press down on one corner of each element to see which one is more stable, less likely to twist or collapse. Note what you have observed.

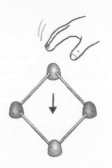
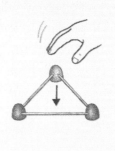

3. Start your dome construction by using five gumdrops and five toothpicks to form the base. Notice that you have made a pentagon, a five-sided figure.

4. Next, use two toothpicks and one gumdrop to make your first triangle on one side of the base.

5. Repeat all the way around the base until you have five triangles.

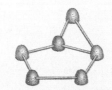
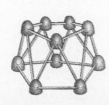
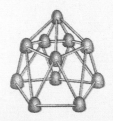

6. Connect the five gumdrops at the top with five toothpicks, as you did in making the base. You should now have a total of 10 triangles.

7. Use toothpicks to connect the gumdrops at the tops of the triangles. Push one toothpick into each of the top gumdrops.

8. Use the last gumdrop to connect these toothpicks at the top.

9. Press down lightly, but firmly, on the top gumdrop. See how stable your dome is. Note how many triangles you have in all.

10. Notice that from the base upward, every element is a triangle.

11. Think about the triangle as a construction element. Explain in your own words why the triangle is so much stronger than a square. As you go about your day, look for examples of buildings and structures where triangle construction can be seen.

Others disagreed. Justice Ruth Bader Ginsburg, in her dissent, declared: "For a half century a concerted effort has been made to end racial discrimination in voting. Thanks to the Voting Rights Act, progress once the subject of a dream has been achieved and continues to be made. The court errs egregiously [badly] by overriding Congress's decision."

Representative John Lewis, a Democrat from Georgia and a longtime leader in the civil rights movement, claimed that the Voting Rights Act was needed now more than ever. "Before the ink was even dry" on the Supreme Court's decision, he said, "states began to put into force efforts to suppress people's voting rights."

Congress Forever Changed

IN THE decades that followed the Voting Rights Act of 1965, African Americans rushed to the polls in increasing numbers. Thousands of black officials were elected across the South. In the process, the Democratic Party, having championed the right of African Americans to vote, gained their allegiance. Many white voters in the South, angry over the civil rights laws now on the books and bound to be enforced, turned to the Republican Party.

The impact of what Congress had done in passing the Civil Rights Act of 1964 and the Voting Rights Act of 1965 went beyond the South. The federal government now had the power, through the Equal Employment Opportunity Commission (EEOC), to vigorously combat employment discrimination, not only in the South but throughout the nation. Title VI of the Civil Rights Act reshaped education. It opened doors for minorities by threatening to withhold federal funds

African American legislators in the 41st and 42nd Congress of the United States.

Library of Congress LC-DIG-ppmsca-17564

to educational institutions that discriminated. And a new civil rights law passed in 1968, known as the Fair Housing Act, helped integrate neighborhoods.

Not surprisingly, Congress itself changed, too. More African Americans were elected to the House and even the Senate.

A look at the 113th Congress (2013–2014) shows just how far diversity in the federal legislature has come. When one adds up women, African Americans, Hispanics, Native Americans, and Asian Americans, there are now more minorities on the Democratic side of the House aisle than white males (nearly 60 percent). With Republicans, the number of nonwhite males in the House actually fell from 14 percent in 2010 to 12 percent in the 113th Congress. However, there were three Hispanic Republican senators (all Cuban Americans) in the Senate. Furthermore, an African American Republican senator, Tim Scott, took to the Senate in 2013. Scott was the first black person to represent a southern state since 1881.

While 68 percent of the House of Representatives is still white and male, there is no denying an overall improvement in elected diversity, a trend likely to continue. Looking back, when Rosa Parks said she was tired of giving in, little did she know what would come of it—a civil rights revolution that the Congresses of the 1960s brought to fruition.

★ SHIRLEY CHISHOLM ★

Shirley Chisholm, courageous, strong-willed, and assertive, was the first African American woman to serve in the US Congress. "Just wait, there may be some fireworks," she said upon being elected to the 12th Congressional District in Brooklyn, New York, in 1968. Her campaign slogan had been "Unbought and unbossed." Indeed, in her seven terms in Congress (1969–1982), Representative Chisholm was never afraid of a good fight. She championed equal rights for women, the Equal Rights Amendment to the Constitution, extension of the minimum wage to domestic workers, and federal day-care facilities. Chisholm was an unabashed liberal who would "fight the good fight" every day she remained in Congress.

Congresswoman Shirley Chisholm announcing her candidacy for the presidential nomination, January 25, 1972.
Library of Congress LC-DIG-ppmsc-1264

When Chisholm first arrived as a member of the House of Representatives, she immediately challenged the **seniority** system. That system had placed her on the Agriculture Committee—an assignment she felt was not relevant to an urban district like hers. "Apparently all they know here in Washington about Brooklyn is that a tree grew there," she said, referring to the 1943 novel *A Tree Grows in Brooklyn*, where a tiny, lonely tree was seen growing out of a brick wall. Before long, Chisholm was transferred to the Veterans Affairs Committee and eventually to the Education and Labor Committees.

Born in 1924, in the poverty-ridden Bedford-Stuyvesant district of New York, Chisholm demonstrated her gutsy style soon after she learned to walk. "Mother always said that even when I was 3, I used to get the 6- and 7-year-old kids on the block and punch them and say, 'Listen to me.'"

"I'd like them to say that Shirley Chisholm had guts," the congresswoman told James Barron of the *New York Times*. "That's how I'd like to be remembered." Shirley Chisholm died at her home in Ormond Beach, Florida, on New Years Day, 2005. She was 80 years old.

Modern Civil Rights and Congress

GIVEN THE magnitude of the struggle for equal rights that African Americans have been striving for since gaining their freedom from slavery, their fight, and the role Congress has played in it, have largely defined civil rights in the minds of Americans for many years. However, civil rights has a much broader spotlight today, where advancement of equality for all people, regardless of race, sex, age, disability, national origin, religion, or sexual orientation (or sexual identity) is being actively pursued.

In the early 1970s, the proposed Equal Rights Amendment (ERA) to the US Constitution was intended to guarantee equality to all persons regardless of gender. It passed the Congress in 1972. However, the amendment did not receive enough votes for ratification by the individual states (it fell three states short). Thus the ERA was never signed into law.

The Americans with Disabilities Act (ADA), passed by Congress in 1990, protects employees from discrimination on the basis of a disability. Under the act, employers are required to make "reasonable accommodations" for their employees' disabilities.

Before President Bill Clinton signed the law that became known as "Don't Ask, Don't Tell" (DADT) in 1993, it was illegal for members of the military to be gay. DADT was designed to protect the privacy of gay people serving in the military; with its passage, homosexuals serving in the military were not allowed to talk about their sexual orientation. They were not permitted to engage in sexual activity. Commanding

President Barack Obama signs into law the Don't Ask, Don't Tell Repeal Act of 2010. Wikimedia Commons

officers were not allowed to question service members about their sexual orientation. DADT was designed to change discriminatory policy, but many gay rights activists criticized DADT. They felt it forced gay people into secrecy and did not go nearly far enough in granting true equal rights for gay individuals to serve in the military. In December 2010, both the House of Representatives and the Senate voted to repeal the policy. On December 22, President Barack Obama signed the legislation.

In February 2004, President George W. Bush called for a constitutional amendment to ban same-sex marriage nationwide. The president, and his supporters, wanted what was known as the Defense of Marriage Act (DOMA) to become the law of the land. Under such an amendment, marriage would be defined as a union between a man and a woman. The proposed amendment has been introduced in Congress. As of this writing, no vote has been taken.

Individuals who are designated as lesbian, gay, bisexual, transgender, queer, and/or questioning their sexual identity fall into a category known as LGBT. At this time, workplace discrimination on the basis of one's actual or perceived sexual orientation is not explicitly prohibited by federal law. Most in the LGBT community hope to someday get Congress to forbid such discrimination.

Members of the Senate Judiciary Committee confer during hearings before the committee on Capitol Hill in Washington, Saturday, Oct. 12, 1991 to investigate the allegations of sexual harassment by Clarence Thomas brought by Anita Hill. From left are: Charles Grassley, R-Iowa, Alan Simpson, R-Wyo, Arlen Specter, R-Pa., Orrin Hatch, R-Utah, and Strom Thurmond, R-S.C.

AP Photo/John Duricka

HAVING OUR SAY
Congress—Advise and Consent

On Saturday, August 24, George Washington, his presidency but a few months old, went to seek advice and consent from the US Congress. Knowing that the Constitution required him to obtain Senate approval of any treaty he negotiated, the president appeared at the Senate chamber on Capitol Hill. Washington had with him a series of proposed US–Indian nation treaties. The president read the documents aloud and asked the Senate's consent. There was dead silence. Finally, several senators asked that they be given time to inform themselves on the matter and put off further discussion until Monday.

The delay "defeats every purpose of my coming here," fumed Washington, who had wanted immediate approval of his treaties. He never sought advice and consent in person again, although the requirement remained. Indeed, it would be 130 years before another president of the United States, Woodrow Wilson, would himself deliver a treaty to the Senate.

According to Article II, Section 2, of the Constitution:

[The president] shall have Power, by and with the Advice and Consent of the Senate, to make Treaties, provided two thirds of the Senators present concur; and he shall nominate, and by and with the Advice and Consent of the Senate, shall appoint Ambassadors, other public Ministers and Consuls, Judges of the supreme Court and all other Officers of the United States . . .

In other words, the US Senate has the exclusive right to provide advice and consent to the president on (1) treaties and (2) nominations. Providing consent is clear: a majority vote of the Senate confirms a nomination; a two-thirds vote is necessary to approve a treaty. What giving advice means, however, is less obvious.

In actuality, the Senate does not ratify treaties. Instead, it takes up a resolution of ratification (approval), by which the Senate formally gives its advice and consent, empowering the president to proceed with the treaty.

When it comes to presidential appointments to the executive and judicial branches, the Senate either accepts or rejects, by a majority of senators present and voting.

Since 1789, the Senate has rejected only 21 treaties. The Senate has confirmed 95 percent of all cabinet nominations. But it has spurned a third of all those nominated to the Supreme Court. Senators accept that presidents deserve advisers who agree with them. Besides, they know such appointees will not stay beyond the president's term. With the judiciary, where good-behaving members hold office for life, senators are more cautious with their approval.

Reservationists and Irreconcilables

WORLD WAR I was known as the Great War. Fought from 1914 to 1918, an estimated 8.5 million were killed and another 21 million wounded. The United States, which entered the war only in the last two years of battle, nevertheless lost 116,000 soldiers. Germany, the main European power fighting against the Allies (made up primarily of Britain, France, and the United States) suffered severely—2 million of its citizens died. Europe in 1919 was a ravaged continent, its survivors demoralized and its infrastructure of transportation and communications destroyed.

It is little wonder that the European Allies, having suffered so much from a war that the defeated Germany had started, would be in a less than charitable mood. Speaking for the United States, President Woodrow Wilson wanted Germany punished, too. But he insisted it be

Design a Congressional Medal of Honor

THE CONGRESSIONAL MEDAL OF HONOR is the highest US military decoration awarded for bravery and valor in action "above and beyond the call of duty." It is awarded to men or women serving in the armed forces of the United States. The medal is generally presented to its recipient by the president of the United States in the name of the US Congress. In this activity, you will select a Congressional Medal of Honor recipient from the Congressional Medal of Honor Society website, write a short profile of the honoree, and design a medal specifically for that person.

Materials

* ★ Access to a computer with a printer
* ★ Pencil
* ★ Poster board, 11 × 17 inches (279 × 432 millimeters)
* ★ Glue stick
* ★ Medal template (make a photocopy onto a sheet of white paper)
* ★ Colored felt, pencils, crayons, or markers
* ★ Scissors
* ★ Embellishments such as beads, feathers, foam shapes, yarn, tiny trinkets

1. Go to the Congressional Medal of Honor Society website at www.cmohs.org. Go to "Recipients." Choose one of the categories: "Full Archive," "Living Recipients," "Recent Recipients," "Recently Departed," "Double Recipients," or "Featured Recipient."

2. Choose a recipient by clicking on the word "view" to the far right of his or her listing. Peruse the profile information. If this is the honoree you want to feature, print out the information. If this is not the individual, keep searching.

3. Open a Word document and write out the basic information on your recipient, such as Name, Organization, Company, Division, etc. You may also want to paste the website photograph of the recipient into your Word document. In your own words, write a short, one-paragraph statement on what the honoree did to earn the Congressional Medal of Honor.

4. Print out the document and paste it onto the lower half of your poster board.

5. Create a pen or pencil drawing inside the circle on the photocopy you made of the five-star medal. The image should depict the main event that illustrates why your honoree was awarded the Congressional Medal of Honor. If, for example, a navy man rescued people from a burning ship under combat fire, your drawing might depict that scene.

6. Use appropriate colors to enhance the meaning of your drawing. Remember that white represents purity and innocence; red represents hardiness, valor, and blood; and blue signifies vigilance, perseverance, and justice.

7. Enhance the ribbon on your medal drawing. One possibility is to depict 13 stripes symbolizing the original 13 colonies.

8. You may want to place a symbol at the tip of each point on the star. A cluster of laurel leaves could represent victory. A cluster of oak will depict strength. You might want to add embellishments to your medal to produce a 3-D effect. Be creative; enhance your medal in any way that furthers the story of your Congressional Medal of Honor recipient.

9. Cut your medal artwork out and paste it onto the top half of your poster board. Your teacher may want you to stand up in class and present your Congressional Medal of Honor. It will be interesting to see how your fellow students interpret your design.

done in a way that would lead to European reconciliation as opposed to revenge. Wilson set sail for Europe, arriving in January 1919, to present his views to the victorious Allies meeting at the Palace of Versailles, near Paris.

Months later, on his return to the United States, Wilson demanded that the Senate accept the treaty he had helped negotiate in Europe—known as the Treaty of Versailles. However, with a Democratic president facing a Republican-controlled Congress (one led by Senator Henry Cabot Lodge of Massachusetts), winning Senate acceptance would not be easy.

Lodge was a brilliant man, with a law degree and a PhD from Harvard University. But upon being elected to the House of Representatives in 1886, and taking a Senate seat in 1893, he became a partisan Republican. In the Senate he rose to leadership of the Foreign Relations Committee. Lodge spent little energy on domestic issues. Foreign affairs were his chief concern. Many came to think of Lodge as the first unofficial Senate majority leader. The senator would spend his 31 years in the Senate defending its privileges, insisting that the Constitution gave clear guidelines as to what the Senate could and could not do.

Democrats mostly supported the treaty. Republicans were divided. Lodge led a group of senators known as the Reservationists. They called for approval of the treaty only if certain alterations, or reservations, were adopted. One provision of the treaty that most upset the Reservationists was the requirement that all members defend any other member who might become the target of aggression. Lodge believed this provision undermined American sovereignty. He insisted that only Congress, and not the League of Nations, an entity set up by the treaty, could commit American troops to war.

Senator William E. Borah, of Idaho, led another group of Republicans who considered

Dignitaries gathered in the Hall of Mirrors at Versailles to sign the peace treaty ending World War I, June 28, 1919. Library of Congress LC-DIG-ppmsca-7634

themselves Irreconcilables. For them it was simple—they were opposed to the Treaty of Versailles under any circumstances.

Attempts were made between the administration and Congress to compromise, but to no avail. Much of the failure rests with President Wilson. In a tactical error that would be inexcusable in today's political climate, the president hadn't taken a single Republican legislator with him to the negotiations in Europe. For Wilson, it was an all-or-nothing deal—my way or the highway.

In the end, the Republicans in Congress won. For the first time in history, the Senate rejected a peace treaty. By a vote of 39 to 55, those supporting the treaty fell far short of the two-thirds majority needed for approval. The United States never ratified the Treaty of Versailles and it did not join the League of Nations. Instead, in 1921, Congress approved a resolution formally ending hostilities with Germany.

The Odd Sound of His Name

THE NOMINATION of a Supreme Court justice is a complex process, one that requires the nominee to jump through many hoops and over a number of hurdles.

First, the president nominates an individual. The Federal Bureau of Investigation (FBI)

★ FILIBUSTER AND CLOTURE ★

The **filibuster**, used in the US Senate, is a delaying tactic to block legislation. It dates from the very first Congress. From that time forward, senators have felt it important that every member have the ability to speak for as long as necessary on any subject.

In one of the most famous filibusters, Senator Huey P. Long (Democrat from Louisiana) held the floor for 15 hours. In his filibuster, Long both frustrated and entertained the Senate by reciting Shakespeare, the Bible, and recipes for "pot-likker" (a southern dish). Then in 1957, Strom Thurmond (who began his senatorial career as a Democrat but switched to the Republican Party in 1964 in opposition to the civil rights movement) filibustered the Senate for over 24 hours—a record.

Filibusters take place at the state level as well as nationally. On June 25, 2013, state senator Wendy Davis (Democrat from Texas) filibustered for 11 hours. Despite her filibuster and the surrounding media firestorm, the bill ultimately passed.

Until 1917, the Senate had no way of ending a filibuster. Upon the urging of then President Woodrow Wilson, the Senate adopted a rule that permitted a two-thirds vote of the Senate to end debate, thus invoking **cloture**, or a time limit on the filibuster. Today, it takes only three-fifths, or 60 votes, to do the same.

---

does exhaustive background checks. And the American Bar Association evaluates the nominee's judicial qualifications. All this takes place before the Senate takes any action toward providing advice and consent.

Second, the nominee must complete lengthy questionnaires, from both the Justice Department and the Senate Judiciary Committee. It could be months before the nominee is finally called before the Senate.

Launch a Petition Action

THE RIGHT TO PETITION the government (Congress) to correct something you think is wrong is written into the US Constitution. In a petition, one makes a formal, written request to government officials stating dissatisfaction with an issue one wishes them to address. Petitioning, like boycotting, protesting, marching, demonstrating, and lobbying, is a way to have your voice heard. In this activity, you will form groups in class that will plan for a "petition action." Your group will go through the steps of assembling and petitioning for a "redress of grievances" and will present the group's work to the class. Later, when you are older, you might want to take the petitioning of Congress to its full conclusion.

Materials
★ Access to a computer with a printer
★ Poster board, 11 × 17 inches
★ Glue stick
★ Scissors
★ Magazines, brochures, fliers, greeting cards, etc.
★ Colored felt pens, crayons, or markers

1. Your teacher will divide the class into groups, each with five or six students.

2. As a group, do some research to find three or four quotations that illustrate "activism," "action," and "empowerment." For example, "Action is an antidote [remedy] to despair" (Joan Baez, singer and songwriter). Keep the quotes handy while your group proceeds with the activity.

3. Have your group brainstorm (mull over) issues of social concern and injustice in schools or the local community. Prepare a list of half a dozen.

4. Have the group vote on the issue they would like to make the focal point of their petition.

5. Research the issue. As your group does this, ask the following: Who do you want to benefit from your work? What are the important publications or websites about your topic? Who in your community might come and speak about the issue? Come up with a list of five or six important points about the issue chosen.

6. Ask yourself, "Who will NOT be happy that you're taking on this issue?" Make a list of four or five common arguments against the issue of your petition. Come up with counterarguments.

7. Prepare an action plan. In doing so, ask yourself the following questions: What is your ultimate goal? What do you want to see changed or happen? How will you get to your goal? What methods will you use to achieve the goal? What steps can you take to get the maximum publicity for your topic? Will you enlist the help of local radio, television, and newspapers? Will you begin a letter-writing campaign? Who will you write to and why?

8. Using poster board as a base, prepare a collage presentation to the class of your action plan. Use words, pictures and drawings, and embellishments to illustrate the answers to the questions in Steps 6 and 7.

9. Present your petition drive results to your class. Were there any challenges in obtaining signatures? Discuss with the class.

Judge Robert Bork, appointed in 1987 by President Ronald Reagan to replace Justice Lewis Powell on the Supreme Court, made it to the Senate Judiciary Committee—no problem. No one ever doubted his credentials to sit on the nation's highest court. Robert Bork had been a judge on the US Court of Appeals. He served as solicitor general (a person who represents the federal government before the Supreme Court). And he was acting attorney general during the Nixon administration. Judge Bork was smart and experienced enough to be an associate Supreme Court justice. It was his politics, his ideology, that for many was the problem.

On the same day that Reagan announced he would nominate Bork, Senator Edward Kennedy of Massachusetts signaled that this would not be an easy confirmation for the judge. In a lengthy opening sentence, Kennedy said:

Robert Bork's America is a land in which . . . blacks would sit at segregated lunch counters, rogue police could break down citizens' doors in midnight raids, school children could not be taught about evolution, writers and artists could be censored at the whim of the government, and the doors of the federal courts would be shut on the fingers of millions of citizens.

Judge Bork's judicial record was exhaustive, and there was a long, detailed paper trail of just what he believed. In a 1963 article, Bork once called civil rights demonstrators "a mob who coerced other private individuals in the exercise of their freedom." Years later, Bork stated, "If I hadn't written anything they [his critics] wouldn't have had anything to distort."

In Judge Bork's defense, attorney Edwin Meese said, "The vicious opposition by the left to Bob Bork's nomination turned what had sometimes been a contentious confirmation process into literally a political campaign."

Bork was an undisputed champion of judicial restraint. The term is primarily associated with the concept of maintaining the status quo.

In contrast, the doctrine of judicial activism implies that the court can and must go beyond a strict interpretation of the Constitution and make judgments in light of changing times.

The Senate Judiciary Committee, after lengthy and contentious hearings, all of which were televised, voted 9–5 not to support Bork's nomination. The final Senate vote was 58 to 42— a stinging rejection.

According to one observer, "Mr. Bork's scruffy beard and the odd sound of his surname made him offputting, as did his sometimes-prickly manner."

Many liberals in the Senate were fiercely opposed to Judge Bork because, at the time,

Judge Bork was the undisputed champion of judicial restraint. Bettmann/CORBIS U873812

placing a conservative on the Court would have tipped the balance to the right. Reagan eventually nominated Judge Anthony M. Kennedy to the Supreme Court. His ideology more to the middle, Kennedy was unanimously confirmed by the Senate.

"High-Tech Lynching"

JUDGE CLARENCE Thomas's nomination to the US Supreme Court, by President George H. W. Bush in 1991, was no less contentious than Robert Bork's. The outcome, however, was more pleasing to conservatives. Though the final Senate vote to confirm Thomas (52–48) was by the narrowest margin in a century, he became a Supreme Court associate justice on October 16, 1991.

Not only is Clarence Thomas considered to be the most conservative judge on today's Supreme Court, by many standards he may be one of the most conservative justices to ever serve on the court. Many African American and civil rights organizations, including the NAACP (National Association for the Advancement of Colored People), opposed the Thomas nomination. The legal community also voiced concerns about Thomas, pointing to his lack of experience for the job. He had served only two years as a federal judge.

Still, Clarence Thomas's nomination cleared the Senate Judiciary Committee on September 27, 1991. Though the vote was split 7–7, and the nomination proceeded to the full Senate without a clear recommendation, Thomas had jumped an important hurdle.

Yet, on the first day that the nomination reached the Senate floor the fireworks started. Anita Hill, a 35-year-old law professor at the University of Oklahoma, came forward to accuse Thomas of sexual harassment. Hill described to the hearing (which was, of course, being televised) how her one-time boss, Thomas, had pressured her to go out with him. She said when the two were alone in the office, Thomas had subjected her to sexually explicitly conversations.

Thomas immediately demanded to be heard, to rebut Hill's accusations. Referring to senators before him, Thomas said, "It [the nomination hearing] is a high-tech lynching for uppity blacks who in any way deign to think for themselves, and it is a message that unless you kowtow [submit] to an old order, this is what will happen to you."

In the aftermath of Thomas's confirmation, a number of important developments came about. First, the Supreme Court took a decided turn to the right. It has remained a conservative court to this day.

Clarence Thomas became a US Supreme Court associate justice on October 16, 1991.

Wally McNamee/CORBIS WL8829

Furthermore, the confirmation hearings put the issue of sexual harassment in the workplace front and center on the American stage.

Finally, it became clear that the November elections of 1992 would be the "Year of the Woman." Four new female senators were elected, two of them from California, and the House added 24 women to its chamber. It has been argued that this increase in women legislators may have been a result of female outrage over the treatment of Hill by a male-dominated Senate. By the end of 1992, both conservatives and liberals had something to cheer about.

Despite being a sometimes bumpy process in which presidents don't always get the advice or the consent they would like, advice and consent is an authority given by the US Constitution to the US Senate. Under its terms, the Senate ratifies treaties and confirms high-ranking presidential appointments. The advice and consent requirement is an example of the checks and balances built into the Constitution. The provision is designed to limit presidential power.

★ DIANNE FEINSTEIN ★

Dianne Feinstein was born in San Francisco, California, in 1933. She graduated from Stanford University in 1955, and was elected to the San Francisco Board of Supervisors in 1970. In 1978, Feinstein became the mayor of San Francisco, an office she held for 10 years.

Dianne Feinstein was first elected to the US Senate from California in a special election in 1992, the "Year of the Woman." Her peer, Senator Barbara Boxer, from California, was also elected to the Senate in the same year. California was the first state to send two female senators to Congress at the same time. Both senators are Democrats.

Feinstein has been reelected four times since 1992 and claims the record for the most popular votes in any US Senate election, having received 7.75 million votes in the 2012 election. At age 80 (in 2013) Feinstein is the oldest currently serving US senator.

Senator Dianne Feinstein was mayor of San Francisco before being elected to the US Senate.
Courtesy of Dianne Feinstein

Senator Feinstein has built her Senate career on furthering assault weapon bans, protecting the Mojave Desert, and as an expert on national intelligence. She has served as the chair of the Select Committee on Intelligence since 2009.

★ ★

The Capitol building undergoing restoration in 27. To the left in the picture, the Capitol building is being prepared for the addition of what will become a large, mostly underground, visitor center. Library of Congress LC-DIG-highsm-4923

HILL STYLE AND HOME STYLE
Congress and Campaigning

Congress's approval ratings are down, while members' workloads are up. More and more, individuals and groups are seeking access to their representatives and senators. Members spend increased money and time seeking reelection. And it seems harder and harder for Congress to do what a congress is supposed to do—come together. These are just some of the challenges Congress confronts in the early 21st century.

For years, polls have attempted to gauge what Americans think of their Congress. While there have been a few upticks in approval ratings over the last four decades, for the most part the results have been universally negative, if not downright depressing. In a poll conducted in early January 2013, just 9 percent of the electorate expressed a positive opinion of Congress.

An astonishing 85 percent disapproved of the legislative body. It was the worst showing of any American institution in the history of polling. The military, public schools, banks, organized labor, and health maintenance organizations (HMOs) all ranked higher than Congress.

To further illustrate: root canals, cockroaches, traffic jams, brussels sprouts, and, yes, used car salespeople were given more favorable ratings than Congress.

Why is this so? Why has a democratic institution that has lasted over 200 years fallen into such disregard?

Maybe it's the image, incorrect though it might be, of a Congress that not only doesn't work well but doesn't do much work at all. In Washington, there exists what is known as the "Tuesday through Thursday Club." This phrase refers, at least on the surface, to a congressional workweek consisting of three days and two nights. Members leave town Thursday evening and do not return until late the following Monday night or early Tuesday morning.

In late July 2013, Congress announced that it would take a five-week **recess**, known, officially, as a "summer district work period." In a poll taken on August 7, 2013, only 14 percent of voters thought Congress deserved the summer break. Eighty-two percent did not.

The public's unhappiness with Congress as an institution stems, in part, from the way any legislative body goes about its business. Making laws and deciding how to spend taxpayers' money is a messy and complicated process. Most constituents don't want to hear about all the confusion, bargaining, and compromising. They want government to do its job quietly and effectively, without fuss and bother. But this is not how democracy works.

It is interesting that while Americans have a negative image of Congress as a whole, they do not feel that way about their individual representatives or senators. Before the 2010 midterm elections, public approval of Congress stood at 21 percent. Yet only 31 percent of likely voters said their own member of Congress should *not* be reelected. In 2010, about 85 percent of members seeking reelection were returned to office.

This gap between opinions of Congress as an institution and individual membership may be due, in part, to different expectations for each. Many citizens see "two Congresses"—one that deals with national issues and the other with their own local concerns. For an individual representative or senator, balancing the two can be a challenge.

"A great job for deviant human beings"

THE "TUESDAY through Thursday Club" notwithstanding, members of Congress, 435

Make a House Ceremonial Mace

THE MACE of the House of Representatives is an ornamental staff (a walking stick) that symbolizes authority before the legislative body. On the rare occasion that a member becomes unruly, the **sergeant at arms**, upon the order of the Speaker, lifts the mace from its pedestal at the front of the chamber and presents it before the offenders. Order is thus restored. In this activity, you will construct a ceremonial mace. While the actual House Mace has a solid silver eagle atop its globe, yours will have a foam board with the image of any animal that you think best symbolizes the United States of America: its democracy, courage, and strength.

Materials

- ★ 3 wooden dowel rods, ½ inch in diameter, from 3 to 4 feet in length
- ★ Acrylic paints, assorted colors
- ★ Paintbrushes, assorted sizes
- ★ 1 white foam board, at least 6 × 6 inches, 3/16-inch thick
- ★ 1 white Styrofoam ball, 4 inches in diameter
- ★ 2 medium-sized rubber bands
- ★ 6 yards tape, ¾ inch wide, preferably silver
- ★ 1 small black binder clip
- ★ 2 wood screws, either flathead or Phillips (preferably with large head), 1 inch long
- ★ Screwdriver
- ★ White glue

1. Paint the three wooden dowel rods (pole) black their entire length. Set them aside to dry.

2. On one side of the foam board, draw an image of the animal you wish to represent America. Paint the animal using assorted colors. Let your board dry.

3. On the Styrofoam ball, draw an outline and then paint an image of the Western Hemisphere, from top to bottom. This image indicates the front of your mace.

4. Wrap two rubber bands, one on each end, around the three wood dowel rods, held together to form a triangle. The rubber bands are there to temporarily hold the rods in place.

5. Starting at one end, and proceeding at a 45-degree angle, wrap the tape around and down the pole. Then, with a second strip of tape, proceed back up the pole repeating the taping such that in the end you have two crisscrossing pieces of tape.

6. Using the binder clip, grasp the foam board at the bottom center.

7. Place the binder clip at the top of the Styrofoam ball and spread the two chrome springs out. Mark their location on the ball and, using the two screws, screw the binder clip in place.

8. Using your screwdriver, gouge out a hole at the bottom of the Styrofoam globe. This is where you will insert the pole. Don't make the hole too big. You want the pole to fit tightly into the hole. The hole should be at least an inch deep.

9. Work the pole into the hole, twisting as you insert it.

10. Apply a generous amount of glue surrounding the hole to secure the pole in place. Let the glue dry.

Display your House Ceremonial Mace. Compare your mace with others made in the class. Wherever you go with the mace, you are now the sergeant at arms.

representatives and 100 senators, work long, hard hours. One may complain about what they do or what, if anything, they accomplish, but there can be little doubt that they put in the time.

To begin with, there are many formal work groups, mainly committees, that every member of Congress must commit to. The average senator sits on three full committees and seven subcommittees. Representatives average two committees and four subcommittees. Furthermore, in a typical Congress, more than 1,000 votes are recorded in the House and close to 600 in the Senate. Congresswoman Debbie Wasserman-Schultz, Democrat of Florida, feels no need to work out in the House gym. "I get my exercise running around the Capitol," she said. "In Congress," adds former Representative Pat Schroeder, Democrat from Colorado, "you are a total juggler. You have always got seventeen things pulling on your sleeve."

In a survey of both House and Senate members, 45 percent gave "inefficiency" as the thing that most surprised them about Congress. "[Congress] is a good job for someone with no family, no life of their own, no desire to do anything but get up, go to work, and live and die by their own press releases," said former Representative Fred Grandy, an Iowa Republican. "It is a great job for deviant human beings."

One reason for the increased workload is, ironically, the relative ease with which one can travel back and forth from Washington to the home district, thanks to jet travel. In addition, with the advent of air-conditioning on Capitol Hill, an individual can at last work through the muggy days of summer. Today, congressional sessions span most of the year.

Going back and forth, from the Hill to home, taking care of national needs and constituents, is something that adds to the workload and stress of anyone having to do it. As a retiring House committee chairman remarked, "One problem is that you're damned if you do and damned if you don't. If you do your work here [Washington], you're accused of neglecting your district. And if you spend too much time in your district, you're accused of neglecting your work here."

Again, there are two Congresses. One is the Congress on Capitol Hill, where national issues are debated and decided and where laws are made. The other is the representing Congress, in which congresspeople serve voters back home. A member of Congress is always thinking, *What must I do for my constituents to get the votes I need to be reelected?* Congresspeople must serve both needs—they must have a "Hill style and a home style."

The two Congresses are, of course, intertwined. A member of Congress was once asked, "Sometimes it must be hard to connect what you do here [at home] with what you do in Washington?" "Oh no," the lawmaker replied. "I do what I do here [in my district] so I can do what I want to do there [in Washington]."

Seeking Access

IN SEEKING to both satisfy constituents and perform their legislative duties, members of Congress find that they have power. That power stems from the ability to pass or defeat legislation and the power to spend money on various projects. Thus it is not surprising that interest groups, from labor unions, corporations, colleges and universities, charities, churches, environmental groups, senior citizens organizations, and even local, state, and foreign governments, seek access in an attempt to influence the decisions members of Congress make.

Such interest groups hire lobbyists whose job it is to convince members of Congress to support their clients' activities. The lobbying profession is a legitimate part of the democratic political process. It is a protected activity under the US Constitution that guarantees rights to free speech, assembly, and to petition the government. Lobbying is a regulated industry.

While there is little doubt that lobbying took place in the very first Congress, the term itself did not come into wide use until the 1820s. Lobbyists often worked the halls or lobbies of

An illustration from 1900 shows "Justice" being buried under an avalanche of legislation.
Library of Congress LC-DIG-ppmsca-25384

91

Visit a Congressional District Office

ALL MEMBERS OF CONGRESS, both senators and representatives, have at least one district office. The staff, also known as caseworkers, seek to solve constituents' problems in dealing with the federal bureaucracy. If a social security check is missing, a veteran's claim is held up, or political asylum (protection) is sought, it is the congressional caseworker who will attempt to solve the problem. In this activity, you will visit your representative's district office to interview a caseworker. In doing so, you will want to obtain examples of casework having been completed, whether the outcome was successful or not. Here, from Congressman Michaele Capuano, of the 7th congressional district of Massachusetts, is an example of casework with a positive outcome:

Case 10: Positive Outcome: *A child became ill within days after American adoptive parents took the baby from an orphanage in the former Soviet Union. The cold became pneumonia and tests confirmed HIV [human immunodeficiency virus, the virus that causes acquired immunodeficiency syndrome (AIDS)]. The parents called our office, and a series of very good events happened quickly. The father flew home from former Soviet Union and met with doctors at Children's Hospital who produced a treatment plan.... The happy healthy toddler has visited my office.*

Materials

★ Access to a computer with a printer
★ Paper and pen or pencil for taking notes

1. Go to your representative's website and obtain the contact information regarding his or her district office.

2. Write to the district director. If he or she is not mentioned, write directly to the member of Congress. Send a letter by e-mail or regular post.

3. In your letter, explain briefly that you wish to set up an appointment with a caseworker, to interview the worker regarding what he or she does. Ask for approximately 30 minutes of the caseworker's time.

4. If you do not get an immediate response, do not be discouraged. Be persistent, but *always* be courteous.

5. Once a date and time has been arranged, confirm your appointment a day ahead of time. Be sure to note the name and title of the specific caseworker you will be seeing.

6. Prepare a set of questions you will be asking the caseworker and send them to him or her ahead of time. A half-dozen questions should do it.

7. Arrive 15 minutes early for your scheduled interview. Dress in nice clothing. In interviewing the caseworker, try to take good notes. Ask for an example of a case that had a positive outcome, one that had a negative outcome, and one that was neutral in outcome. Keep in mind, you do not need (nor will you be given) the actual name of a particular individual—that information must remain confidential.

8. As you leave the district office, be sure to thank the caseworker you talked to and anyone else you met. When you return home, immediately send a thank you message to the caseworker.

9. Prepare a one-page report, detailing one or two cases you learned about. The report should place all the congressional office details at the top, to be followed by the name of the caseworker you interviewed.

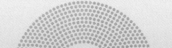

the House and Senate chambers. They sought to buttonhole (grab) members of Congress or their staff, face them eye to eye, and get them to listen to their pleas. That process continues to this day, in spite of all the new technology available to lobbyists interested in engaging members of Congress. Being there physically still has the maximum effect.

Lobbying is not well understood by the general public. It has come to have a sinister image, given the various scandals associated with its activities. In 2006, a lobbyist named Jack Abramoff pleaded guilty to fraud, tax evasion, and conspiracy to bribe public officials. In seeking to advance the interests of the gambling industry by means of donations, luxury trips, and favors, Abramoff went way beyond what was legal. "I don't think we have had something of this scope, arrogance, and sheer venality [corruption] in our lifetime," declared Norman J. Ornstein, a longtime Capitol Hill watcher. The resulting scandal ended the political careers of six members of Congress as well as numerous congressional staffers.

In spite of the distrust the public feels toward lawmakers, their behavior is actually more open to public view and members of Congress are more qualified than ever before. The media probes their conduct at every turn. There have been real campaign finance and ethics reforms. All this helps to reduce corruption. It is true, in the old days some lobbyists would walk around with envelopes stuffed with cash to hand out to powerful lawmakers. Today, contacts between lobbyists and lawmakers are open to more scrutiny by reporters and civic groups.

Lobbyists are also seen as extensions of a congressional office staff. They provide information and data and explain sometimes complex issues simply so busy congresspeople and their staffs can understand the issues more easily.

Lobbying, it must be remembered, is a form of free speech. It is performed not only by professional interest groups but also by volunteer citizens seeking to influence members of Congress. The right to speak our mind to our government representatives is one of the most basic freedoms we have.

Pressing the Flesh

It is called opposition research, or "oppo," by various congressional campaigns. Its purpose is "to get the skinny on the client's opponents and, if all goes well, expose them as **hypocrites**, liars, thieves, or just plain unsavory characters." But in a recent election, the challenger for a Senate seat was advised to do something rather startling—turn opposition research on himself. He was told that before he even committed to a campaign to unseat an incumbent senator, he would have to spend $50,000 to hire a firm

Create a Glossary Word Search

ONE OF THE BEST WAYS to familiarize yourself with words in the glossary is to create a glossary word search.

Materials
★ Ruler
★ Graph paper
★ Pencil with an eraser
★ Copy of the glossary starting on page 109
★ Highlighter pen

1. Using a ruler, draw a square on your graph paper. The larger the square, the larger the puzzle, and the more words you will use.

2. Looking at the glossary at the end of this book, pick words that you will put inside the drawn square. As you write the words, use uppercase letters, one per square. You can write the words across, up and down, backward, and diagonally. Choose as many words as you like.

3. To the side of your square, keep a list of the words you are using so that players can know what to look for.

4. After you have written in all the words that you will want a player to find, fill in the blank squares with letters. Wherever possible, use short letter combinations that are part of some of the words you used.

5. Players should identify a word with a highlighter pen.

As a player identifies a word, he or she can read over the glossary definition.

that would dig up all the dirt it could—on him. Thus, it was hoped, armed with everything that could be thrown at him, the challenger would be ready.

Welcome to the world of campaigning for Congress in the 21st century.

There are many ways those seeking congressional office choose to campaign. There are TV, the Internet, text messages, e-mails, Facebook, Twitter, mass mailings, and professionally staffed phone banks, to name a few. All can be effective. But there is also "pressing the flesh," campaigning door-to-door. Its advantage is its low cost. Indeed, if you are a challenger and short of cash, you might have little choice but to get out there and meet voters the old-fashioned way.

Former Representative Dan Glickman, Democrat from Kansas, describes his first House campaign as follows:

I walked door-to-door to 35,000 homes over an eight-month period. I walked from 10:30 A.M. to 2 P.M. and again from 5:30 P.M. to 8 P.M. I lost 35 pounds and learned to be very realistic about dogs. I met a woman my father had lent $100 or $150 to 30 years before. She embraced me and said, "You saved us." I won by three percentage points.

Commendable and successful as Representative Glickman's efforts were, it is extremely difficult for a challenger to beat a member of Congress already in place—an incumbent. Since World War II ended, in 1945, on average 93 percent of all incumbent representatives and 81.5 percent of all incumbent senators running for reelection have been returned to office.

One reason for this low challenger success rate is the difficulty in finding quality opponents. In some cases, party leaders can't locate candidates to run at all. In 2010, 27 incumbent House members ran unopposed, as did one senator.

A key strategy for an incumbent is to scare off opposition by building up a giant war chest of reelection money. And, not surprising, campaign contributors, sensing that an incumbent is invincible, will pour money into his or her campaign rather than a challenger's.

But a win is not always assured. Incumbents can be beaten. In referring to a threat to her reelection, Representative Pat Schroeder had this to say regarding how effective just one constituent could be:

I've always thought that the tradition of writing a letter to your congressman is a pretty meager idea; what goes on between one government official and one constituent doesn't pack much of a wallop. How much more effective to make a poster that says: "WANTED: Pat Schroeder. This creep does x, y, or z." Then mail it to me with a note that says, "I just made one thousand of these, and I think I'll put them in menus wherever I eat, and elevators, and restrooms, and bus shelters, and the Laundromat . . ." Now you have my attention.

In this illustration, published in 1912, an elephant, representing the Republican Party, is asking a woman, representing the consumer, to fill his "Dinner Pail" with food. But the consumer's basket is empty. The cartoonist was implying that the Republican Party had taxed the necessities of life, such as food, so highly that the consumer had nothing left to give. Library of Congress LC-DIG-ppmsca-27837

★ MARJORIE MARGOLIES ★

It was a phone call freshman Representative Marjorie Margolies will never forget. President Bill Clinton had just assumed office and was facing a massive federal **deficit**. (The government's spending was exceeding its income.) To combat the problem, Clinton proposed a combination of spending cuts and tax increases. The wealthier taxpayers were scheduled to take the largest tax hit.

Every Republican in the House voted against the bill. Yet there were enough conservative Democrats to tie the tally at 217–217. Democratic Representative Margolies, whose district contained a large number of those upscale taxpayers, had originally planned to vote against the bill. But then Bill Clinton called. The president pleaded with Margolies for her vote. He told her his presidency depended on it. Margolies gave her vote to the president, and the 1993 budget authorization passed the House.

When Margolies reluctantly voted "yes," she heard other representatives crying out, "Bye-bye, Marjorie." They were right. Margolies lost her bid for reelection in 1994. "Do you represent or do you lead?" the freshman representative declared later. "In the end, one must put aside all the chatter, noise, all the headlines, all the calls, close the door to your office, and make a very tough and often unpopular choice."

Margolies has tried numerous comebacks. In 1998, she ran for lieutenant governor of Pennsylvania. She won the Democratic primary but lost the general election.

That defeat has not defeated Margolies, however. On May 31, 2013, at age 70, she filed the necessary paperwork to run in the Democratic Party primary for a return to Congress in 2014 from her old district. Margolies could have one major advantage: the Clinton family. Her son is married to Chelsea Clinton.

Marjorie Margolies is again running for Congress.
Wikimedia Commons

Representative Schroeder won all her reelection bids.

Even though 95 percent of all House members are reelected, there is turnover in each election. At any given moment, half the representatives will have served less than 11 years. Senators, to be sure, are accustomed to longer tenure.

Coming Together

THE WORD "Congress" comes from the Latin for "coming together." Today, there seems little effort on the part of members to work together, or to compromise on major issues confronting the nation. While polls repeatedly show citizens supporting their individual representatives and senators, Congress as an institution receives low marks—a failing grade. Yet, in the eyes of the public, our national legislative body has had rough going almost from the start. In 1925, Nicholas Longworth, Speaker of the House, remarked:

> *During the whole of that time [throughout history] we have been attacked, denounced, despised, hunted, harried, blamed, looked down upon, excoriated [censored], and flayed. I refuse to take it personally. I have looked into history. . . . We were unpopular when Lincoln was a congressman. We were unpopular when John Quincy Adams was a Congressman. We*

were unpopular even when Henry Clay was a congressman. We have always been unpopular. From the beginning of the Republic, it has been the duty of every free-born voter to look down upon us, and the duty of every free-born humorist to make a joke at us.

Congress's image has not been helped by what the public perceives as arrogance and dishonesty on the part of many members. Referring to her early years in Congress, Representative Pat Schroeder declared:

There were days I thought I was on the Mississippi River because of all the showboating [showing off] in Congress. We were 435 class presidents, unleashed into the world beyond high school. Everyone was so afraid of becoming a follower that no one agreed with anyone else. People stole each other's bills and reintroduced them rather than co-sponsoring them. We dealt with such pressing issues as whether it was legal to fly a kite in the District and whether policemen would allow firemen to play in their band.

Is it any wonder the public has become disenchanted and cynical about the US Congress?

Dr. Samuel Johnson (1709–1784) supposedly said, regarding a dog's walking on its hind legs, "It is not done well; but you are surprised to find it done at all." So it is with the US Congress. The institution has survived for over two centuries. It is far older than most of the world's existing governments. It is all we have. In creating the Congress, our framers did a remarkable thing. It is up to us as citizens to keep it going. We do that by insisting on accountability from our congresspeople. And accountability will occur if we get and stay involved.

Winston Churchill, Britain's World War II prime minister, famously stated, "No one pretends that democracy is perfect or all-wise. Indeed, it has been said that democracy is the worst form of government except all those other forms that have been tried from time to time."

The US Congress, as our founding fathers intended, is a reflection and fulfillment of our democracy. As a representative institution, it is us.

✫ ✫ ✫ ✫ ✫ ✫ ✫ ✫ ✫ ✫ ✫ ✫ ✫ ✫ ✫ ✫ ✫ ✫ ✫ ✫

As a senator from Missouri, Harry Truman championed legislative oversight with regard to national defense programs.

AFTERWORD

We live in a very special country. The United States of America is a place where people believe that everyone should have a voice. It is a nation where "We the People" choose our representatives; with our votes, we can hold them accountable for their decisions.

There are many times in our nation's history when Congress's decisions have changed the way our country works as well as transformed how the world operates.

When existing law was unfair, Congress abolished slavery and gave women the right to vote. When we needed to promote economic development, Congress created an interstate transportation system so businesses could get their products to consumers more easily. When our soldiers are stationed overseas, Congress helps equip them with the tools they need to protect themselves and our country.

The Constitution assigns a number of responsibilities to Congress, but its authority is not unlimited. While the executive and judicial branches have a duty to keep Congress in check, the most important check on Congress is you.

Even if you're too young to vote, you can still write, call, or e-mail your members of Congress. Let them know what issues matter most to you. Take the time to learn as much as you can about our government, about Congress, and about being a good citizen.

When you turn 18, study the candidates running in your area and make your voice heard on Election Day. And maybe one day, members of your community will elect you as their representative in Congress and you can have the privilege—and responsibility—of being their voice in our nation's capital.

REPRESENTATIVE KRISTI NOEM has served in the House of Representatives since 2011, representing South Dakota's at-large congressional district. She is known for championing small business, entrepreneurs, and farmers.

WEBSITES TO EXPLORE

US Capitol Visitor Center

www.visitthecapitol.gov

THIS IS your link to the US Capitol Visitor Center. In order to visit Capitol Hill in person, you must enter via the center. This website takes you on a virtual tour of the actual center. At the website you can plan your visit, see numerous exhibitions, and, of course, learn about the Capitol and Congress. Of particular interest is the link to Special Activities and Tours. If you plan an actual visit to the Capitol, this website should be your first stop. If you don't plan to go to Washington, all the more reason to take this virtual Capitol tour.

Congress.gov

http://beta.congress.gov

THIS IS the home page for the US Congress. It will give you the current legislative activity for the entire Congress. You can access the *Congressional Record* from this website. You can do a bill search to locate current bills pending in Congress. This is an excellent starting point to find out what is going on in the current Congress.

Library of Congress

www.loc.gov

THIS IS the Library of Congress (LOC) home page. The site features webcasts from the LOC, numerous topics to explore, and a section for "Kids & Families." Of course, anything you want to know about the LOC itself is here. And this is the place to begin your in-depth research on anything about the US Congress. This is an informative and fun website to explore.

GovTrack.us Research Congress

www.govtrack.us/congress

THIS WEBSITE is excellent for tracking legislation in the US Congress, including members of Congress, bills and resolutions, voting records, and committee activities—it is all here. With regard to members of Congress, the site has a directory going back to the founding of our nation. As to Bills & Resolutions, one can track the status of all bills in Congress from introduction to enactment. The Voting Records section tracks the votes of members of Congress on bills and procedural motions from 1789 to the present.

Congress for Kids

www.congressforkids.net

DESIGNED FOR students in grades four through high school, this site insists that learning about the federal government need not be boring. According to its authors, "Using appealing, full-color illustrations, and engaging activities, this site will extend your learning in the basics about the American federal government." With Congress for Kids, you will learn more about all three branches of the federal government in an interactive, fun-filled way.

Government for Kids

http://kids.usa.gov/government/index.shtml

THIS IS an excellent website for kids grades K–5, teens grades 6–8, and even for grown-ups. On this site you can play games and watch videos in addition to reading concise, easy-to-understand explanations for just about anything having to do with the US government. Much of the site is interactive, allowing you to explore a subject in a fun manner.

A Kid's Guide to the United States Congress

http://articles.usa-people-search.com/content-a
 -kids-guide-to-the-united-states-congress.aspx

THIS WEBSITE reminds the viewer that "The laws that Congress pass have an effect on everyone, even on kids! They tell us what is legal, or what we can and cannot do, just like parents in a way." The site links dozens of resources about the US government, with an emphasis on Congress. Congress Explained for Kids, Election Game, PBS Kids' Democracy Project, Kids Voting USA Website, How an Idea Becomes a Law, and US Government Games are just some examples.

NOTES

Chapter 1

"You have libeled my state" McNamara, "Violence Over Slavery on the Floor of the US Senate."

"Of course he has chosen a mistress" Senate Historical Office, "The Caning of Senator Charles Sumner."

"This damn fool [Sumner] is going to get" McNamara, "Violence Over Slavery on the Floor of the US Senate."

"*The Migration or Importation*" US Constitution, Article I, Section 9.

"South had won a great victory" Finkelman, *The Abolition of the Slave Trade*, 3.

"probably the most important slavery" Miller, *Arguing About Slavery*, 20.

"The relations which now exist" Senate Historical Office, "March 16, 1836: Gag Rule."

"We took each other" Remini, *The House*, 41.

"What do the petitioners ask" Miller, *Arguing about Slavery*, 52.

"to petition the Government" Remini, *The House*, 129.

Chapter 2

"Job creation and renewable energy" Haglage, Dickson, and Keller, "U.S. Politics: Meet the Freshmen: Introducing the New Members of the 113th Congress."

"If men were angels" Ritchie, *The Congress of the United States*, 47.

"was adopted by the Constitution" Ritchie, *The Congress of the United States*, 203.

"The House should have an immediate" Davidson, Oleszek, and Lee, *Congress and Its Members*, 8.

"Why did you pour that coffee" Zelizer, *The American Congress*, 24.

"The nine largest states are home" Davidson, Oleszek, and Lee, *Congress and Its Members*, 45.

"Members regularly complained" Remini, *The House*, 16.

"They're already making money" Bolton, "Warren Ruffling Feathers in Clubby Senate," *The Hill*, July 20, 2013, 1.

"I love her, she is a dear" Ibid., 2.

"They've done a wonderful job" Ibid.

Chapter 3

"The President, Vice President" US Constitution, Article II, Section 4.

"powerful legislative check" Senate Historical Office, "Impeachment."

"An impeachable offense is whatever" Senate Historical Office, "Impeachment."

"state suicide" Benedict, *The Impeachment and Trial of Andrew Johnson*, 63.

"I repose in this quiet" Stevens, *The Biography Channel* website, www.biography.com /people/thaddeus-stevens-21011351.

"Edmund Ross in particular" Benedict, *The Impeachment and Trial of Andrew Jackson*, 124.

Chapter 4

"He [Reed] was one of the few men in public life" Remini, *The House*, 245.

"a deafening mass of individuals yelling" Remini, *The House*, 248.

"For some minutes there was" Ibid.

"I deny your right, Mr. Speaker" Ibid.

"The Chair is making a statement" Ibid.

"The House of Representatives shall chuse" US Constitution, Article I, Section 2.

"To be a senator" Zelizer, *The American Congress*, 358.

"As suffragists pled their cause" Senate Historical Office, "September 30, 1918: A Vote for Women."

"We have made partners of the women" Senate Historical Office, "September 30, 1918: A Vote for Women."

"As a woman" Alter, *Extraordinary Women of the American West*, 153.

"I took the dearest" Dewhirst, *Encyclopedia of the United States Congress*, 425.

Chapter 5

"He doesn't stand a Chinaman's chance" "1882: American Sinophobia, The Chinese Exclusion Act and 'The Driving Out,'" Sacramento's Chinatown Mall.

"the good order of certain" *The Chinese Exclusion Act (1882): Brief Overview*, 1. www .lehigh.edu/~ineng/VirtualAmericana/ chineseimmigrationact.html.

"America's present need is not" Cohen, "Senator Warren G. Harding—Return to Normalcy Speech," *Live from the Campaign Trail*. http://livefromthetrail.com/about

-the-book/speeches/chapter-3/senator
-warren-g-harding.

"the most important turning-point" Higham,
Strangers in the Land, 311.

"would virtually disappear" *U.S. Congress,
House, 1964 hearings*, 418.

"yet to hear a single proponent" ProCon.
org, "Top 10 Pros and Cons: Illegal
Immigration." http://immigration.procon
.org/view.resource.php?resourceID=000842
&print=true.

"I witnessed the trials" Simon, "Immigration
divides GOP colleagues," *Los Angeles Times*.

"We do not need more" Ibid.

"I am on my way to" Spencer, "Dreamers'
dreams," Spencer, *Guardian*.

"Currently I am in graduate school" Ibid.

"I hope to take advantage of" Ibid.

"crown prince of the Tea" *Telegraph UK*,
"Midterms 2010: Tea Party 'Crown Prince'
Marco Rubio Wins", www.telegraph.co.uk
/news/worldnews/us-politics/8106646
/Midterms-2010-Tea-Party-Crown-Prince
-Marco-Rubio-wins.html.

"*They have come because*" "Sen. Marco Rubio
Speaks From the Heart for Immigration
Reform," ABCNews.com, http://abcnews.
go.com/blogs/politics/2013/06/sen-marco
-rubio-speaks-from-the-heart-for
-immigration-reform/.

Chapter 6

"To investigate the extent, character" Remini,
The House, 322.

"I have in my hand a list" History Matters.
"'Enemies from Within': Senator Joseph
R. McCarthy's Accusations of Disloyalty."
http://historymatters.gmu.edu.

"the brains of a five-year-old" Dewhirst,
Encyclopedia of the United States Congress, 345.

"not fit to wear that uniform" Ritchie, *The
Congress of the United States*, 19.

"traitors and communists" Dewhirst,
Encyclopedia of the United States Congress, 346.

"Until this moment, Senator" Giblin,
The Rise and Fall of Senator Joseph McCarthy,
239.

"Have you no sense of decency" Dewhirst,
Encyclopedia of the United States Congress, 346.

"What happened?" Ibid.

"third-rate burglary" "Senate Select
Committee on Presidential Campaign
Activities (The Watergate Committee",
www.senate.gov/artandhistory/history
/common/investigations/Watergate.htm.

"Sandy Alderson, a senior Major League
official" Committee on Oversight and
Government Reform.

"extensive media coverage" Ibid.

"As a sport, we have done everything" Ibid.

Chapter 7

"Judge Smith's graveyard" Breitzer, "Civil Rights Act of 1964," *Encyclopedia Virginia*, 3.

"separate but equal" McElrath, Jessica, African-American History, About.com.

"The right of citizens of the United States" 15th Amendment to the US Constitution, Section I.

"receive clearance from the Justice" Liptak, "Supreme Court Invalidates Key Part of Voting Rights Act" *New York Times*, June 25, 2013, 3.

"Our country has changed" Liptak, "Supreme Court Invalidates Key Part of Voting Rights Act," *New York Times*, June 25, 2013, 2.

"For a half century" Ibid.

"Before the ink was even dry" Koseff, "Hearing reveals a partisan split over voter rights ruling," *Los Angeles Times*, July 18, 2013, A6.

"Just wait, there might" Barron, "Shirley Chisholm, 'Unbossed' Pioneer in Congress, Is Dead at 80," *New York Times*, January 3, 2004.

"Apparently all they know " Ibid.

"Mother always said that" Ibid.

"I'd like them to say" Ibid.

Chapter 8

"defeats every purpose" Ritchie, *The Congress of the United States*, 12.

"[The president] shall have Power" US Constitution, Article II, Section 2.

"Robert Bork's America is a land" Sherman, "Robert Bork Nomination Fight Altered Judicial Selection." www.huffingtonpost.com/2012/12/19/robert-bork-nomination_n_2332933.html.

"a mob who coerced other" Feeney, "Robert Bork, 85; nomination to US Supreme Court prompted bitter battle." *Boston Globe*, December 20, 2012.

"If I hadn't written anything" Sherman, "Robert Bork Nomination Fight Altered Judicial Selection."

"The vicious opposition" Ibid.

"Mr. Bork's scruffy beard" Ibid.

"It [the nomination hearing] is a high-tech lynching" Totenberg, "Thomas Confirmation Hearings Had Ripple Effect" *NPR*, October 11, 2011.

"Year of the Woman" Dewhirst, *Encyclopedia of the United States Congress*, 505.

Chapter 9

"summer district work period" Remini, *The House*, 499.

"Tuesday through Thursday Club" Ibid.

"I get my exercise running" Davidson, Oleszek, and Lee, *Congress and Its Members*, 120.

"In Congress, you are a total juggler" Schroeder, *24 Years of House Work . . . and the Place Is Still a Mess*, 76.

"[Congress] is a good job" *Washington Post*, October 18, 1994, B3.

"One problem is that you're damned" Louviere, "For Retiring Congressmen, Enough Is Enough," *Nation's Business,* May 1980, 32.

"Sometimes it must be hard" Fenno, *Home Style: House Members in Their Districts*, 99.

"Case 10" Capuano, "Examples of Casework and Constituent Assistance Provided by Congressman Capuano's Office," http://www.house.gov/capuano/services /casework_examples.shtml.

"I don't think we have" Ornstein, "The Abramoff Saga: The Worst Hill Scandal in Our Lifetime?" *Roll Call*, October 19, 2005, 5.

"to get the skinny on the client's" Sabato and Simpson, *Dirty Little Secrets*, 156.

"I walked door-to-door" Zipkin, "Landing the Job He Wanted," *New York Times*, April 17, 2005, C10.

"I've always thought that the tradition" Schroeder, *24 Years of House Work . . . and the Place Is Still a Mess*171.

"During the whole of that time" Ritchie, *The Congress of the United States*, 60.

"There were days I thought" Schroeder, *24 Years of House Work . . . and the Place Is Still a Mess*, 34.

"It is not done well" The Samuel Johnson Sound Bite Page. www.samueljohnson .com/dogwalk.html.

"No one pretends that democracy" Thinkexist. com. en.thinkexist.com/quotation/it_has _been_said_that_democracy_is_the_worst _form/15815.html.

GLOSSARY

advice and consent Presidential nominations for executive and judicial posts take effect only when confirmed (given consent) by the Senate. International treaties become effective only when the Senate approves them by a two-thirds vote.

amendment A proposal to change the text of a pending bill by striking out some of it, by inserting new language, or both.

bill The way lawmakers introduce their proposals (enacting or repealing laws, for example); they address either matters of general interest ("public bills") or narrow interest ("private bills"). An example of the latter would involve immigration cases and individual claims against the federal government.

bipartisanship Cooperation, agreement, and compromise between two major political parties.

Capitol The building where the US Congress meets.

capital The place where the federal government resides. It is located in Washington, DC.

checks and balances The feature by which power is distributed across the three branches of government so that each branch checks the others.

cloture The only procedure by which the Senate can overcome a filibuster. It is done by voting to place a time limit on consideration of a bill. Today, it takes three-fifths of the full Senate, 60 votes, to invoke cloture.

committee A group of representatives or senators established by the rules of its respective chamber. It is here that issues are considered and legislation prepared.

Congressional Record The proceedings on the House or Senate floor. It is printed for each day the House or Senate is in session.

constituency A body of citizens entitled to elect a representative, as to a legislature.

Constitution The legal document laying out the structure of the US federal government and its powers.

deficit The amount by which spending exceeds income. (A surplus would be the amount by which income exceeds spending.)

districts Each state is divided into congressional districts. The number of districts in a state is determined by the state's population. Each district elects one representative to serve in the House of Representatives.

filibuster A term for any attempt to block or delay Senate action on a bill by debating it at length, offering numerous procedural motions, or by any other delaying or obstructive actions.

floor Action "on the floor" is that which occurs as part of a formal session of the full House or Senate. A representative or senator who has been recognized to speak by the chair is said to "have the floor."

founding fathers The early political leaders of the United States.

government The leadership of a community, state, or nation.

House chamber The room where the House of Representatives meets.

hypocrite A person who acts in contradiction to his or her stated beliefs.

impeachment To accuse someone of misconduct. Only the US House of Representatives can impeach.

incumbent The holder of an office.

laws Rules of conduct established and enforced by a government entity.

legislative day A "day" that starts when the Senate meets after an adjournment and ends when the Senate next adjourns. Hence, a legislative day may extend over several calendar days or even weeks and months.

Library of Congress "America's Library," the Library of Congress is the largest library in the world. It is located on Capitol Hill.

majority leader The majority leader is elected by his or her party conference to serve as the chief House or Senate speaker for the majority party and to manage and schedule the legislative and executive business of the two branches.

majority whip Party leaders in the House and Senate responsible for maintaining party discipline and cohesion are known as whips.

mandate An order to act given to a representative.

minority leader See majority leader. The minority leader is the speaker for the party not in power.

minority whip The minority parties in the House and Senate have whips that function as do majority whips.

morning hour A time in both the House and Senate when formalities and routine business transpire.

partisan Firmly committed to a cause, faction, or party.

peculiar institution The institution of slavery in the South.

president pro tempore An officer of the Senate who presides over the chamber in the absence of the vice president. The president pro tempore ("president for a time") is elected by the Senate and is, by custom, the senator of the majority party with the longest record of continuous service.

quorum The number of members of the House or Senate, or their respective committees, required to be present to do business. The number is usually 50 percent of those who should be attending plus one.

ratify To approve formally, to confirm.

recess With regard to the Senate, a temporary interruption of its proceedings, sometimes within the same day. The Senate may also recess overnight rather than adjourn at the end of the day. Recess also refers to longer breaks, such as the breaks taken during holiday periods.

roll call vote A vote in which each member votes "yea" or "nay" as his or her name is called by the clerk, so that the names of the members voting on each side are recorded.

Senate chamber The room where the Senate meets.

senator A person elected or appointed to the Senate and duly sworn in. A senator must be at least 30 years old, a citizen of the United States for at least nine years, and an inhabitant of the state from which he or she is elected.

seniority The status given representatives and senators according to their length of service. As a representative or senator gains seniority, he or she is given preferential treatment in matters such as committee assignments.

sergeant at arms Both the House and Senate elect a sergeant at arms to enforce the rules and regulations and to oversee the protection of members, staff, and visitors.

subcommittee A subgroup of members of a committee. Both the House and Senate have many subcommittees that hold hearings or consider legislation.

Tea Party Tea is an acronym for "Taxed Enough Already." The Tea Party is made up of conservatives who want to substantially reduce the role of government while seeking to balance the national budget.

veto The procedure established under the Constitution by which the president refuses to approve a bill or joint resolution and thus prevents its enactment into law. A veto can be overridden only by a two-thirds vote in both the House and the Senate.

BIBLIOGRAPHY

★ Denotes sources most suitable for young readers.

Abramoff, Jack. *Capitol Punishment: The Hard Truth about Washington Corruption from America's Most Notorious Lobbyist.* New York: WND Books, 2011.

Africans in America: America's Journey through Slavery. Part I, 1450–1760—The Terrible Transformation. WBGH, 1998.

★ Aikman, Lonnelle. *We, the People: The Story of the United States Capitol.* Washington, DC: National Geographic Society, 1970.

★ Allen, G. William. *History of the United States Capitol: A Chronicle of Design, Construction, and Politics.* Honolulu: University Press of the Pacific, 2005.

Alter, Judy. *Extraordinary Women of the American West.* New York: Children's Press, 1999.

Ambrose, E. Stephen. *Nothing Like It in the World.* New York: Simon & Schuster Paperbacks, 2000.

★ Barron, James. "Shirley Chisholm, 'Unbossed' Pioneer in Congress, Is Dead at 80." *New York Times.* January 3, 2005. www.nytimes.com/2005/01/03/obituaries/03chisholm.html?_r=0.

Beamon, Todd, and John Bachman. "Rep. Steve King Slams Norquist Over Attacks on Immigration." Huffington Post Politics. www

.huffingtonpost.com/2013/08/01/cantaloupes -congress_n_3689432.html.

Bendiner, Robert. *Obstacle Course on Capitol Hill*. New York: McGraw-Hill Book Company, 1964.

Benedict, Les Michael. *The Impeachment and Trial of Andrew Johnson*. New York: W. W. Norton & Company, 1973.

Bernstein, Carl, and Bob Woodward. *All the President's Men*. New York: Simon & Schuster, 1974.

BrainyQuote. www.brainyquote.com/quotes /authors/n/natham_hale.html.

Breitzer, S. "Civil Rights Act of 1964." *Encyclopedia Virginia*. www.EncyclopediaVirginia .org/Civil_Rights_Act_of_1964.

Cogan, Marin. "Allen West Gets Brushback from Veteran Bishop." Politico's on Congress: Congressional News and Analysis Blog, December 21, 2010. www.politico.com/blogs /glennthrush/1210/Allen_West_gets _brushback_from_veteran_Bishop.html.

Committee on Oversight and Government Reform. "Committee Holds Hearings on Steroids in Baseball." http://oversight-archive .waxman.house.gov/story.asp?ID=816

Constitution of the United States, The. Washington, DC: National Center for Constitutional Studies, 2010.

Constitutional Rights Foundation. "History Lesson 1: History of Immigration through the 1850s." 2012. http://testimmigration .crf-usa.org/index.php/lessons-for-teachers /71-immigrant-article-1.html.

Davidson, Roger H., Walter J. Oleszek, and Frances E. Lee. *Congress and Its Members*. Washington, DC: CQ Press, 2012.

Dewhirst, E. Robert, editor. *Encyclopedia of the United States Congress*. New York: Facts on File, 2007.

Dillingham Commission Reports, The. www .ebrary.com/stanford/Dillingham1.html.

★ Dodge, Andrew. *A Young Person's Guide to the United States Capitol*. Washington, DC: U.S. Capitol Historical Society, 2009.

★ Dodge, Andrew. *Exploring Capitol Hill: A Kid's Guide to the U.S. Capitol and Congress*. Washington, DC: U.S. Capitol Historical Society, 2001.

Dudley, William, editor. *Political Scandals: Opposing Viewpoints*. San Diego: Greenhaven Press, Inc., 2001.

"1882: American Sinophobia, The Chinese Exclusion Act and 'The Driving Out.'" Sacramento's Chinatown Mall. www.yeefow.com/past/1882.html.

"'Enemies from Within': Senator Joseph R. McCarthy's Accusations of Disloyalty." History Matters. http://historymatters.gmu.edu/d/6456.

Feeney, Mark. "Robert Bork, 85; nomination to US Supreme Court prompted bitter battle." *Boston Globe*, December 20, 2012. www.bostonglobe.com/metro/obituaries/2012/12/19/robert-bork-conservative-jurist-dies/AZsY5vQPov9H1xZjj0oLKK/story.html.

Fenno, Richard F. Jr. *Home Style: House Members in Their Districts*. Boston: Little, Brown, 1978.

Finkelman, Paul. The Abolition of the Slave Trade: U.S. Constitution and Acts. http://abolition.nypl.org/print/us_constitution/.

★ Giblin, James Cross. *The Rise and Fall of Senator Joe McCarthy*. New York: Clarion Books, 2009.

Goldman, T. R. "The Influence Industry's Senior Class," *Legal Times*, June 16, 1997.

Haglage, Abby, Caitlin Dickson, and Michael Keller. "U.S. Politics: Meet the Freshmen: Introducing the New Members of the 113th Congress." Daily Beast. www.thedailybeast.com/articles/2013/01/08/meet-the-freshman-introducing-the-new-members-of-the-113th-congress.html.

Hamilton, Charles V. *Adam Clayton Powell, Jr.: The Political Biography of an American Dilemma*. Lanham, MD: Cooper Square Press, 2001.

Higham, John. *Strangers in the Land: Patterns of American Nativism, 1860–1925*. New Brunswick, NJ: Rutgers University Press, 1962.

Hopwood, Jon C. "Baseball and Politics: Congress Investigates Use of Steroids and Other Performance-Enhancing Drugs (Again)." Yahoo! Contributor Network, February 14, 2008. http://voices.yahoo.com/baseball-politics-congress-investigates-of-906243.html.

"Immigration to the United States." Harvard University Library Open Collections Program. http://ocp.hul.harvard.edu/immigration/dillingham.html.

Johnson, Sara. "Diversity in the 113th Congress Looks Pathetic When You Plot It on a Map." The Atlantic Monthly Group. www.theatlanticcities.com/politics/2013/01/diversity-113th-congress-looks-pathetic-when-you-plot-it-map/4348/.

★ Kennedy, John F. *Profiles in Courage*. New York: HarperPerennial, 2006.

Koseff, Alexei. "Hearing reveals a partisan split over voter rights ruling." *Los Angeles Times*, July 18, 2013.

★ Lazarus, Emma. "The New Colossus," Statue of Liberty National Monument. www.libertystatepark.com/emma.htm.

Lindsay, James M. "TWE Remembers: Sen. Arthur Vandenberg's Conversion to Internationalism." Council on Foreign Relations. January 10, 2011. http://blogs.cfr.org/lindsay /2011/01/10/twe-remembers-sen-arthur -vandenberg%E2%80%99s-conversion-to -internationalism/.

Liptak, Adam. "Supreme Court Invalidates Key Part of Voting Rights Act." *New York Times*, June 25, 2013. www.nytimes.com/2013 /06/26/us/supreme-court-ruling.html?page wanted=all.

Louviere, Vernon. "For Retiring Congress-men, Enough Is Enough." *Nation's Business*, May 1980.

Lund, M. John. "Boundaries of Restriction: The Dillingham Commission." *University of Vermont History Review* 6: December 1994. www.uvm.edu/~hag/histreview/vol6 /lund.html.

Mackenzie, Alvin G., and Michael Hafken. *Scandal Proof: Do Ethics Laws Make Government Ethical?* Washington, DC: Brookings, 2002.

Maury, William B. *Washington D.C. Past and Present: The Guide to the Nation's Capital*. New York: CBS Publications, 1975.

McElrath, Jessica. African American History. www.afroamhistory.about.com.

McNamara, Robert. "Violence Over Slavery on the Floor of the US Senate." About.com: 19th Century History. http://history1800s .about.com/od/abolitionmovement/a /sumnerbeaten.htm.

★ Miles, Kathryn. *All Standing: The Remark-able Story of the* Jeanie Johnson, *the Legendary Irish Famine Ship*. New York: Free Press, 2013.

Miller, Scott. *The President and the Assassin: McKinley, Terror, and Empire at the Dawn of the American Century*. New York: Random House Trade Paperbacks, 2011.

Miller, William Lee. *Arguing about Slavery: The Great Battle in the United States Congress*. New York: Alfred A. Knopf, 1996.

Moore, John L., editor. *Congressional Ethics: History, Facts, and Controversy*. Washington, DC: Congressional Quarterly Inc., 1992.

Myers & Associates. "Lobbyist & Lobbying." www.meyersandassociates.com/lobbyist.html.

Okrent, Daniel. *Last Call: The Rise and Fall of Prohibition*. New York: Scribner, 2010.

Ornstein, Norman J. "Prosecutors Must End Their Big Game Hunt of Politicians." *Roll Call*, April 26, 1993.

Ornstein, Norman J. "The Abramoff Saga: The Worst Hill Scandal in Our Lifetime?" *Roll Call*, October 19, 2005.

Peacock, Nelson. "Obama's trump card on immigration." *Los Angeles Times*, August 1, 2013. http://articles.latimes.com/2013/aug/01/opinion/la-oe-peacock-immigration-deportation-house-20130801.

Remini, V. Robert. *The House: The History of the House of Representatives*. New York: HarperCollins Publishers, 2006.

★ Ritchie, Donald A. *The Congress of the United States: A Student Companion*. New York: Oxford University Press, Inc., 2006.

Ritchie, Donald A. *The U.S. Congress: A Very Short History*. New York: Oxford University Press, Inc., 2010.

"Rosa Parks." Biography Channel. www.biography.com/people/rosa-parks-9433715.

Rubin, Jerry. *A Yippie Manifesto*. www.montgomerycollege.edu/Departments/hpolscrv/yippiemanifesto.html.

Sabato, Larry J., and Glenn R. Simpson. *Dirty Little Secrets: The Persistence of Corruption in American Politics*. New York: Times Books, 1996.

Schroeder, Pat. *24 Years of House Work . . . and the Place Is Still a Mess: My Life in Politics*. Kansas City: Andrews McMeel Publishing, 1998.

Senate Historical Office. "Advise and Consent." www.senate.gov/reference/reference_item/advise_and_consent.htm.

Senate Historical Office. "Arthur Vandenberg: A Featured Biography." www.senate.gov/artandhistory/history/common/generic/Featured_Bio_Vandenberg.htm.

Senate Historical Office. "Classic Senate Speeches: Thomas Hart Benton." www.senate.gov/artandhistory/history/common/generic/Speeches_Benton1850.htm.

Senate Historical Office. "March 16, 1836: Gag Rule." www.senate.gov/artandhistory/history/minute/Gag_Rule.htm.

Senate Historical Office. "Impeachment." www.senate.gov/artandhistory/history

/common/briefing/Senate_Impeachment _Role.htm.

Senate Historical Office. "May 19, 1856: The Crime against Kansas." www.senate.gov /artandhistory/history/minute/The_Crime _Against_Kansas.htm.

Senate Historical Office. "Senate Select Committee on Presidential Campaign Activities (The Watergate Committee)." www .senate.gov/artandhistory/history/common /investigations/Watergate.htm.

Senate Historical Office. "September 30, 1918: A Vote for Women." www.senate.gov/artand history/history/minute/A_Vote_For_Women .htm.

Senate Historical Office. "The Caning of Senator Charles Sumner." www.senate.gov /artandhistory/history/minute/The _Caning_of_Senator_Charles_Sumner.htm.

Sherman, Mark. "Robert Bork Nomination Fight Altered Judicial Selection." Huffington Post. www.huffingtonpost.com/2012/12/19 /robert-bork-nomination_n_2332933.html.

Simon, Richard. "Immigration divides GOP colleagues." *Los Angeles Times*, July 28, 2013.

Spencer, Ruth. "Dreamers' dreams." *Guardian*, July 12, 2012. www.theguardian.com/world /interactive/2012/jul/12/dreamers-dreams -young-immigrants-interactive.

"The Chinese Exclusion Act (1882): Brief Overview." www.lehigh.edu/~ineng /VirtualAmericana/chineseimmigrationact .html.

Thinkexist.com http://thinkexist.com /quotation/it_has_been_said_that _democracy_is_the_worst_form/15815.html.

"Timeline of the Revolutionary War." UShistory.org (Independence Hall Association), 1999–2013. www.ushistory.org /declaration/revwartimeline.htm.

"Top 10 Pros and Cons: Illegal Immigration." ProCon.org. http://immigration.procon.org /view.resource.php?resourceID=000842& print=true.

Totenberg, Nina. "Thomas Confirmation Hearing Had Ripple Effect." *NPR*, October 11, 2011. www.npr.org/2011/10/11/141213260 /thomas-confirmation-hearings-had-ripple -effect.

Uslaner, Eric M. *The Decline of Comity in Congress*. Ann Arbor: University of Michigan Press, 1993.

"Vermont Representative William Slade's Antislavery Speech in the 25th Congress."

United States House of Representatives: History, Art & Archives. http://history.house.gov/HistoricalHighlight/detail/36690.

Waxman, Henry. *The Waxman Report: How Congress Really Works.* New York: Hachette Book Group, 2009.

Samuel Johnson Sound Bite Page. www.samueljohnson.com/dogwalk.html

Youth International Party. www.bookrags.com/Youth_International_Party.

Zelizer, Julian E., editor. *The American Congress: The Building of Democracy.* New York: Houghton Mifflin Company, 2004.

Zipkin, Amy. "Landing the Job He Wanted," *New York Times,* April 17, 2005.

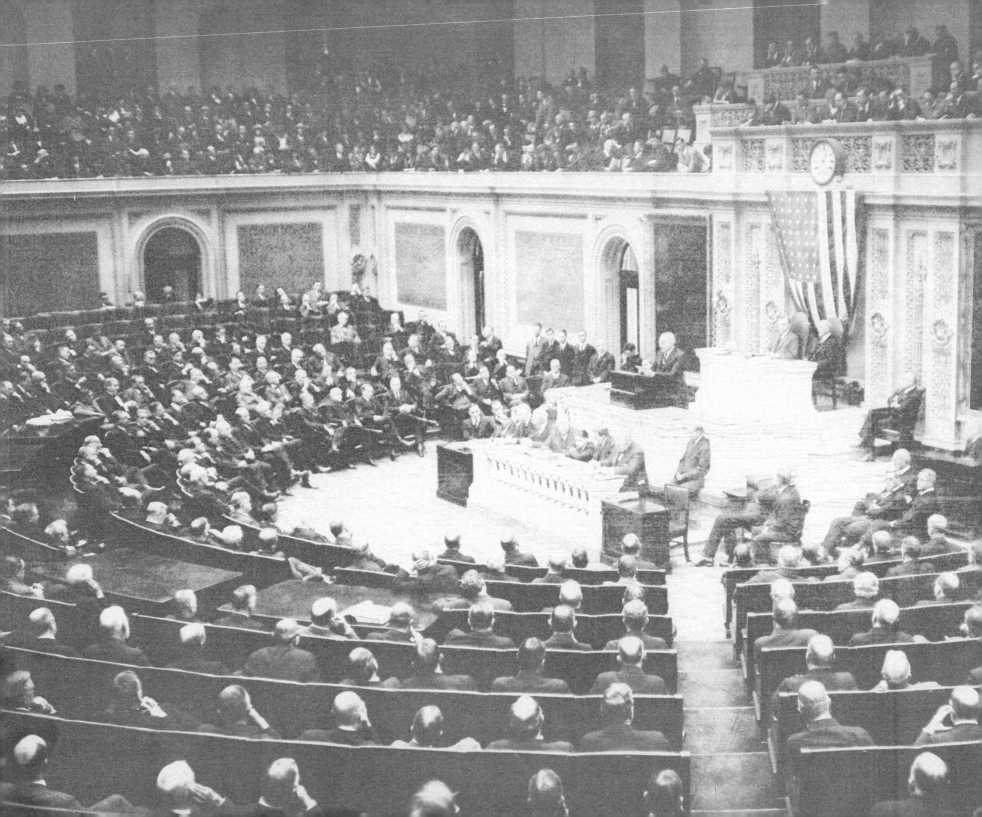

INDEX

Page numbers in **bold** refer to illustrations; page numbers in *italics* refer to definitions

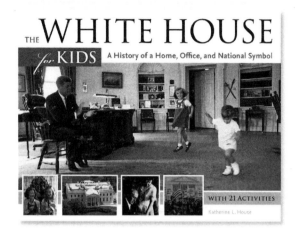